Flora vitiensis ?a description of the plants
of the Viti or Fiji islands, with an account of
their history, uses, and properties /By Berthold
Seemann; ... plates by Walter Fitch. Volume v. 2

Fitch, W. H., Seemann, Berthold,

the drawing (Plate X) of a large frond of Forster's *P. scandens* instead of the true species, and he has misled all subsequent observers. The following is the synonymy of the species:—*Pleopeltis pustulata*, Carr ms, non Moore. *Polypodium pustulatum*, Forst Prodr. n 136 (*fide* Herb Forst.), non Schkuhr, Willd. nec auct alior. *P. scandens*, Labill. Nov. Holl vol ii p. 91 t. 210, non Forst *P. diversifolium*, Willd Sp. Pl vol ii. p 166, non R. Br *P. Billardieri*, R Br Prodr p 147; Hook. Sp. Fil vol. v p. 82

XXXVII. **Dipteris**, Reinwardt, Syllogr. Pl. Nov. (1828), vol. ii p. 3. Sporangia inter venas primarias dichotomas earumque divisiones, venulis anastomosantibus insidentia, in soros subrotundos sparsos collecta. Venæ dichotomo-glabelliformes, venulis prominentibus divaricatissimis crebre anastomosantibus, ultimis v. penultimis soriferis, ultimis apice vix dilatato libero —Filices rhizomate repente; frondibus elongato-stipitatis, binatis, coriaceis.

1. **D. conjugata**, Reinw. Syll. Pl. Nov. vol. ii. p. 3; rhizomate repente, squamis rigidis atris subulatis tecto, stipitibus glabris, castaneis, teretiusculis, antice canaliculatis; frondibus binatis, palmatis, coriaceis, glabris, subtus glaucis; segmentis oblongis v. elongatis, sensim acuminatis, grosse serratis; soris minutis —*Polypodium conjugatum*, Kaulf. Wesen. d. Farrkr. p. 104 *P. dipteris*, Blume, Enum. Fil. Jav. p 135. *P. Horsfieldii*, R. Br. Plant. Jav. Rar. p. 1.—Viti (Seemann! n. 734, Harvey!). Also from Aneitum, New Hebrides (M'Gillivray!), Malicola (C. Moore!), Erromango (M'Gillivray!), New Caledonia (Strange! M'Gillivray!).

XXXVIII. **Drynaria**, Bory (subgenus), Ann. Sc Nat vol v (1825), p. 462. Sporangia venulis anastomosantibus imposita, in soros rotundatos magnos collecta. Venæ pinnatæ, prominentes, venulis crebre anastomosantibus, ultimis liberis, divaricatis.—Filices rhizomate repente; frondibus dissimilibus, fertilibus stipitatis pinnatifidis v. pinnatis, segmentis articulatis, sterilibus sessilibus querciformibus

1. **D. Linnæi**, Carr. ms; rhizomate repente, paleis elongatis fibrillosis onusto, stipitibus glabris, subteretibus, alatis; frondibus coriaceis, glabris, viridibus, juxta rachin pinnatifidis, sinubus rotundato-obtusis, segmentis oblongo-lanceolatis, acuminatis, margine callosis, subrepandis; venis primariis e costa pinnatis, secundariis et ultimis repetite et irregulariter anastomosantibus, frondibus sterilibus sessilibus, late ovatis, profunde sinuatis; soris numerosis, parvis, anastomosante v. medio venularum irregulariter impositis —*Polypodium Linnæi*, Bory (excl. syn., Ann. d. Sc Nat 1825, vol. v. p. 464. t. 12).—Viti (Milne! U. S. Expl· Exped.).

This is a very distinct species from *P. quercifolium*, Linn (ex spec typo in Herb Burmann), and is well characterized and accurately figured by Bory, though he erroneously referred it to Linnæus's species This has led to so much confusion that I will give the synonymy of *P quercifolium*, Linn, as far as I have been able to determine it with certainty *P quercifolium*, Linn Sp Pl ed 1 p. 1057, Schkuhr, Crypt Gew. p. 13 t. 13, Swartz, Syn Fil p 32 *P sylvaticum*, Schkuhr, Crypt Gew p 22 t 86 *P Schkuhrii*, Bory, Ann d Sc Nat 1825, vol v p 467 *P morbillosum*, Presl, Rel Hænk fasc 1 p 22 t. 3. f. 3 —This species is recorded by Mr Baker from Viti, but the specimens I have examined belong to *D. Linnæi*, which Mr Baker has properly reintroduced (Syn Fil p 363) as an independent species.

2. **D. diversifolia**, J. Smith, Hook. Journ. 1841, p 397, rhizomate repente, paleis angusto-lanceolatis subulato-acuminatis onusto, denique pruinato; frondibus sterilibus, oblongis, pinnatilobatis; fertilibus stipitatis, lanceolatis, pinnatis; pinnis numerosis, sessilibus, basi cuneatis, inferioribus sterilibus ovato-lanceolatis, superioribus fertilibus linearibus; soris subcostalibus, inter venas laterales solitariis, impressis —*Polypodium diversifolium*, R. Br. Prodr. p 117 *P Gaudichaudii*, Bory, Ann. d. Sc. Nat 1825, vol. v. p. 471. t. 14. *P. speciosum*, Blume, Enum. Pl. Jav. p. 132. *P. rigidulum*, Sw. in Baker, Syn. Fil. p. 368.—Viti (Seemann! n. 733, Sir E. Home!), Matuku

(H.M.S Herald!). Also from New Hebrides, Aneitum (M'Gillivray! Milne!), and Isle of Pines (M'Gillivray!).

Tribus VII. GRAMMITIDEÆ.

XXXIX. **Diclidopteris,** Brack. U. S. Expl. Exped. *Filices*, p. 135. Sporangia venis imposita, in soros lineares continuos in sulcis obliquis depressos collecta. Venæ simplicissimæ, rectæ, liberæ, sporangiferæ, unica inter costam et marginem æquidistante.—Filices rhizomate repente, frondibus simplicibus linearibus

1. **D. paradoxa,** Carr. ms; rhizomate repente, brevi; frondibus numerosis, longissimis, linearibus, acutis, glabris; costa subtus prominente, venis costa parallelibus, sporangiferis, soris continuis, in sulcis altis obliquis impositis —*Pleurogramme? paradoxa,* Fée, Hist Vittariées, p. 58 t. 4. f. 4. *Diclidopteris angustissima,* Brack. U. S. Expl. Exped. *Filices,* p. 135. t. 17. *Vaginularia Junghuhnii,* Mett Fil. Hort. Lips. p. 25 *Monogramme Junghuhnii,* Hook. Sp Fil vol. v. p 123. Viti (Seemann! n. 718 and 914; U. S. Expl. Exped.), Ovalau (Martens, 267, *fide* Fée). Also from Samoa (Powell!).

The following species from tropical Polynesia may be introduced here.—1 *Monogramma subfalcata,* Hook. Sp. Fil. vol v. p. 122. t. 289 A , from New Hebrides (C Moore) 2. *Grammitis Deplanchei,* Baker. Syn Fil. p 322, from New Caledonia (Deplanche, n 5)

XL. **Gymnogramme,** Desv. Berl. Mag. vol. v p 304. Sporangia latere venarum imposita, in soros lineares simplices v furcatos obliquos collecta. Venæ simplices v. furcatæ, venulis liberis — Filices rhizomate brevi recto, frondibus lobatis, pinnatis v. bipinnatis, herbaceis, subtus sæpe ceraceis v lanatis —*Ceropteris,* Link, Sp. Fil. p 141. *Trismeria,* Fée, Gen. Fil. p. 164. *Coniogramme,* Fée, Gen. Fil p. 167. *Pleurosorus,* Fée, Gen. Fil. p. 179.

The following species are also found in tropical Polynesia —1 *G. marginata,* Mett. Ann Sc. Nat ser. 4 vol xv. (1851), p 59, from New Caledonia (Vieillard). 2. *G javanica,* Bl Fil Jav. p. 112, from Sandwich Islands (D Nelson! Macrae! Hillebrand! U S Expl Exped) 3 *G Brackenridgei,* Carr ms (*G tartareum,* Brack non Desv), from Samoa (Powell! U S Expl Exped)

1. **G. decipiens,** Mett. Ann Sc. Nat. ser. 4. vol. xv. p. 60; rhizomate repente, stipitibus fuscis, nitidis; frondibus linearibus v. ovato-lanceolatis, acuminatis, pinnatis v. basi bipinnatis, pinnulis trapezio-oblongis, obtusis, crenato-serratis, v. inferioribus incisis v. pinnatis, lobis obovatis; venis inferioribus flabellatis, superioribus furcatis, soris elongatis, latere venularum impositis.—Viti (Seemann! n. 819) Also from Aneitum, New Hebrides (M'Gillivray! Milne!), New Caledonia (C. Moore! M'Gillivray! Vieillard), and New Ireland (Turner).

XLI **Selliguea,** Bory, Dict. Class. Hist. Nat. vol. vi. p. 587. Sporangia in soros lineares continuos, super mesoneuron oblique cadentes, plures nervillas invadentes collecta. Venulæ anastomosantes, ultimæ liberæ curvatæ —Filices rhizomate repente, frondibus simplicibus raro pinnatifidis v palmato-lobatis, herbaceis v coriaceis.—*Loxogramme,* Presl, Tent. Pter. p. 214. *Colysis,* Presl, Epim. Bot. p. 146.

The following species is also from tropical Polynesia —*Selliguea plantaginea,* Brack U S. Expl Exped *Filices,* p 58, from Tahiti (Nelson! U. S Expl. Exped).

1. **S. caudiformis,** Carr. ms.; rhizomate longe repente, juniori dense paleaceo, deinde denudato; stipitibus elongatis, teretibus, supra sulcatis, basi paleaceis; frondibus coriaceis, glabris, sterilibus, ovato-oblongis, acuminatis, basi acutis, fertilibus elongatis, lineari-lanceolatis, acuminatissimis;

soris magnis, oblongis, inferioribus 2 v. pluribus inter venas pinnatas, superioribus solitariis.—*Polypodium caudiformis*, Blume, Fil. Jav. p. 116. t. 54. f. 2. *Grammitis caudiformis*, Hook Sp. Fil. vol. v p. 158.—Viti (Milne!). Also from Aneitum (M'Gillivray!).

2. **L. lanceolata,** Presl, Tent. Pter. p. 215; rhizomate repente, paleis ovato-lanceolatis acuminatis onusto; stipitibus brevissimis, basi paleaceis; frondibus coriaceis, glabris, lanceolatis, acuminatis, basi attenuatis et longe decurrentibus; venis immersis; soris elongatis, valde obliquis.— *Grammitis lanceolata*, Sw. Syn. Fil. p 22 and 212. *Antrophyum lanceolatum*, Blume, Fil. Jav. p 84. *Silliguea lanceolata*, Féc, Gen. Polyp p. 177. *Silliguea involuta*, Brack. (non Don) U. S. Expl Exped. *Filices*, p. 58.—Viti (Seemann! n. 725; U. S. Expl Exped.). Also from Tahiti (Nelson!) and Solomon Islands (Milne!).

XLII. **Antrophyum,** Kaulf. Enum Fil. p. 197. Sporangia in soros lineares elongatos flexuosos sæpe interruptos immersos raro superficiales collecta. Venæ reticulatæ, areolas elongato-hexagonoideas constituentes.—Filices rhizomate repente, frondibus simplicibus, coriaceis v. membranaceis.—*Polytænium*, Desv. Ann. Soc. Linn. Par. vol. vi. p. 218.

The following species occur in tropical Polynesia in addition to those described:—1. *A. Grevillii*, Balf. Ann. Nat Hist. ser. 2. vol. ii p. 11 pl 1 (*A. angustatum*, Brack), from Tahiti (Menzies! Barclay! Collie! U. S. Expl. Exped. ; Sibbald). 2. *A reticulatum*, Kaulf. Enum. Fil p. 198, from Society Islands (Forster!), Tahiti (Banks and Solander! Collie! Barclay!), Christmas Island (Collie!).

1. **A. plantagineum,** Kaulf. Enum. Fil. p 197; rhizomate brevi, repente; stipitibus elongatis, basi squamis linearibus subulato-attenuatis serratis tectis; frondibus lanceolatis, acutis v. acuminatis, costa evanescente; soris anastomosantibus, immersis.—*Hemionitis plantaginea*, Cavan. Præl. n. 643.—Viti (Harvey!). Also from Erromango (M'Gillivray!), Aneitum, New Hebrides (M'Gillivray!), Tahiti (Barclay! U. S. Expl. Exped.).

2. **A. Lessonii,** Bory, Voy. Coquille, p 254 t. 28. f. 2; rhizomate brevi, repente; stipitibus elongatis, squamis lanceolatis acuminatis remote denticulatis tectis; frondibus ovoideo-elongatis, utrinque attenuatis, ecostatis, integris, coriaceis; soris linearibus, raro reticulatis, immersis.—Viti (Seemann! n. 717). Also from Society Islands (Forster!), Raiatea (Collie!), Mallicollo (Sinclair!), Tahiti (Barclay! Banks and Solander!).

3. **A. subfalcatum,** Brack. U. S. Expl. Exped. *Filices,* p. 65; rhizomate repente, squamis ovato-lanceolatis serratis tecto; frondibus cæspitosis, membranaceis, subcostatis, lineari-lanceolatis, acuminatis, basi angusto-attenuatis, sessilibus; soris anguste linearibus, immersis —*A. Brookei*, Hook. Second Cent. Ferns, pl. 79.—Viti (Græffe! U. S. Expl. Exped., Milne). Also from Samoan Islands (Parker).

4. **A. semicostatum,** Blume, Fil. Jav. p. 110, rhizomate repente, squamis lanceolatis denticulatis tecto, frondibus obovato-lanceolatis, acuminatis, basi attenuatis, stipitatis, membranaceis; soris angustis, rectiusculis, subimmersis.—Viti (U. S. Expl. Exped.). Also from Mallicollo (Sinclair!), Samoa (Powell! U. S. Expl. Exped.), Tahiti (U. S. Expl. Exped.; Durville), New Ireland (Labillardière).

XLIII. **Vittaria,** Smith, Act. Taur. vol. v. p. 413. t. 9. f. 5. Sporangia in sporos lineares continuos sulcis extrorso-marginalibus plus minusve immersos collecta. Venæ obscuræ, simplices, ad marginem fructiferum coalitæ.—Filices rhizomate repente, squamis longis dentatis tecto, frondibus linearibus glaberrimis coriaceis, margine integris.

1 **V. rigida,** Kaulf. Enum Fil. p. 193; rhizomate repente, squamis lanceolatis angustis acuminatis tecto; frondibus fasciculatis, rigidis, coriaceis, elongatis, linearibus, apice acutis, basi angustioribus; soris in margine continuis —*V. elongata,* Sw. Syn. Fil. p. 109 *V. ensiformis,* Sw l. c p. 109.—Viti (Seemann! n. 719 and 720, Græffe!). Also from Sandwich Islands (Banks and Solander! Nelson! Collic! Barclay! Macrae! Strickland! Hillebrand!). Aneitum, New Hebrides (M'Gillivray!), and Mallicolla (Sinclair!).

XLIV. Syngramma, J. Smith, Hook. Journ. 1845, p. 168. Sporangia in soros superficiales lineares subreticulatos collecta Venæ simplices v furcatæ, infra parallelæ, ad marginem anastomosantes.—Filices rhizomate erecto v. repente, frondibus simplicibus membranaceis teneris diplotaxicis, fertilibus longius petiolatis angustioribus.—*Callogramme,* Fée, Gen. Fil p. 169

Besides the species mentioned below, the following occurs in tropical Polynesia —*S. quinata,* Hook Sp Fil vol. v. p 152 t 297, from Solomon's Islands (Milne! n. 579).

1. **S. pinnata,** J. Sm. Hook. Journ. (1845), p 168. t. 7 C, rhizomate repente; stipitibus semiteretibus, basi setosis, frondibus coriaceis, glabris, simplicibus, ternatis v. pinnatis, pinnis lineari-lanceolatis, attenuatis, basi oblique cuneatis, margine cartilagineo leviter undulatis; soris linearibus v reticulatis, interdum rotundatis (var. β.).—*Gymnogramme pinnata,* Hook Sp. Fil. vol. v. p. 151 *G. subtrifoliata,* Hook l c. *Hemionitis elongata,* Brack. U. S. Expl. Exped Filices, p 66 t 8 —Viti (Seemann! n. 715; Harvey! U. S. Expl. Exped.). Also from Erromango (M'Gillivray!) Isle of Jobi (Barclay!).

Var. β. *rotundata.*—Viti (Milne! Græffe!).

XLV. Hemionitis, Linn Syst Nat. ed 1. Sporangia venis anastomosantibus imposita, in soros superficiales lineares reticulatos collecta Venæ uniformes, anastomosantes, areolis elongato-hexagonalibus.—Filices rhizomate erecto v. repente, frondibus cordatis sagittatis palmatis v. pinnatis, coriaceis v. herbaceis.

1. **H. lanceolata,** Hook. Second Cent. Ferns, t. 55; rhizomate repente, pilis ebeneis tecto; stipitibus badiis, nitidis; frondibus coriaceis, ovato-lanceolatis, acuminatis; costa valida subtus prominente straminea nitidissima, venis patentibus, ubique anastomosantibus, areolas oblongas hexagonas formantibus, venis omnibus soriferis.—Viti (Seemann! n. 717, Milne).

Tribus VIII. ACROSTICHEÆ.

XLVI. Acrostichum, Linn. Syst. Nat. ed. 1. Sporangia paginam totam frondis fertilis tegentia, in soros superficiales collecta. Venæ liberæ, parallelæ, furcatæ.—Filices rhizomate repente v rarius scandente squamigero, frondibus simplicibus integris, diplotaxicis, fertilibus sæpe angustioribus.—*Elaphoglossum,* Schott, Gen. Fil. t. 15.

Besides the species described below, the following also occur in tropical Polynesia ·—1 *A pellucidum,* Gaudichaud, 'Bonite,' t. 79 f. 5-7 (*A splendens,* Brack ; *A. micradenium,* Fée), from the Sandwich Islands (Macrae! Hillebrand! Gaudichaud. U. S Expl Exped.). 2. *A. splendens,* Bory in Willd Sp Pl vol v. p 104, from the Sandwich Islands (Nelson! Strickland! Milne! Hillebrand! Macrae! etc.). 3 *A æmulum,* Kaulf Enum. Fil. p 63 from the Sandwich Islands (Chamisso, Hillebrand! U S Expl Exped). 4 *A glabratum,* Mett. Ann Sc Nat. ser 4. vol. xv. p 54, from New Caledonia (Vieillard) 5 *A Samoense,* Baker, Syn Fil p 407, from the Samoan Islands (U. S. Expl Exped.) 6 *A Tahitense,* Carr. ms (*Elaphoglossum Tahitense,* Brack.), from Tahiti (Nelson! U S Expl Exped).

1. **A. Feejeense,** Hook. Sp. Fil vol. v. p. 199; rhizomate brevi, crasso, repente, paleaceo; stipitibus semiteretibus, basi paleaceis, fertilibus longioribus; frondibus coriaceis, submarginatis,

utrinque lepidotis, sterilibus oblongo-lanceolatis obtusis basi anguste attenuatis, fertilibus parvis oblongis obtusis basi leviter attenuatis; venis immersis, parallelis, furcatis.—*Elaphoglossum Feejeense*, Brack. U. S. Expl. Exped. *Filices*, p. 72.—Viti islands, vicinity of Sandalwood Bay, on trees (U. S. Expl Exped.).

2. **A. obtusifolium**, Blume, Enum. Pl. Jav. p 102; rhizomate crasso, brevi, repente, paleaceo; stipitibus semiteretibus, basi paleaceis; frondibus coriaceis, glabris, submarginatis, obscure lepidotis, obovato-oblongis, obtusis, basi attenuatis, fertilibus angustioribus et stipite longioribus; venis impressis, parallelis et furcatis —*Elaphoglossum obtusifolium*, Brack. U. S. Expl. Exped. p. 72.— Viti Islands, Ovalau, on rocks and trees at an altitude of 2000 feet (U. S. Expl. Exped.).

XLVII **Lomariopsis**, Fée, Hist. Acrost. p. 10. Sporangia paginam totam inferiorem frondis fertilis obtegentia. Venæ simplices v. parallelo-furcatæ, liberæ.—Filices rhizomate scandente, frondibus diplotaxibus heteromorphis pinnatis.

1. **L. Brackenridgei**, Carr. ms.; rhizomate stipitibusque paleaceis; frondibus pinnatis, pinnis alternis, brevi-stipitatis; sterilibus glabris, supra nitidis, lanceolatis, acuminatis, basi attenuatis, margine undulatis; fertilibus linearibus; venis prominentibus, simplicibus, raro furcatis —*Stenochlæna variabilis*, Brack (non Fée) U. S. Expl. Exped. *Filices*, p. 76.—Viti (Seemann! n. 711; U. S. Expl. Exped.). Also from Samoan Islands (Powell!).

2. **L. variabilis**, Fée, Hist. Acrost. p. 70; rhizomate repente, flexuoso, stipitibusque paleaceis, frondibus pinnatis, pinnis stipitatis; sterilibus glabris, lanceolatis, acuminatis, basi oblique cuneatis, margine crenato-serratis; fertilibus linearibus, venis prominentibus.—Viti (U. S. Expl. Exped.). Also from Tahiti (Nelson!).

3 **L. Seemanni**, Carr. ms.; rhizomate scandente, cum stipitibus basi paleaceo, stipitibus teretibus, superne subalatis; frondibus pinnatis; pinnis glabris, sterilibus stipitatis, elongato-oblongis v. linearibus, apice abrupte acuminatis, basi acutis, fertilibus elongato-linearibus, apice abrupte acuminatis; venis simplicibus v. furcatis parallelis —*L cuspidata*, J. Smith (non Fée), 'Bonplandia,' vol. ix. p. 261 —Viti (Seemann! n. 712). Also from Aneitum, New Hebrides (M'Gillivray!).

XLVIII. **Stenochlæna**, J. Smith, Hook. Journ. 1841, p. 401. Sporangia paginam totam inferiorem frondis fertilis obtegentia. Venæ ad costam arcuato-anastomosantes, venulis parallelis, simplicibus v. furcatis, liberis —Filices rhizomate scandente, frondibus diplotaxibus pinnatis, pinnis articulatis, basi glanduliferis.—*Lomariobotrys*, Fée, Gen. Fil. p. 45.

1. **S. scandens**, J. Smith, l. c.; rhizomate scandente, nudo; stipitibus glabris, subteretibus, sulcatis; frondibus coriaceis, glabris, pinnatis; pinnis sterilibus, ovato-oblongis, acuminatis, basi cuneatis, margine spinuloso-serratis, serratis v. integris; pinnis fertilibus elongato-linearibus, margine integro revolutis; venis prominentibus, approximatis, parallelis —*Lomaria scandens*, Willd. Sp Pl. vol. v. p. 293.—Viti (Seemann! n. 710).

Stenochlæna Feejeensis, Brack U. S Expl. Exped *Filices*, p 78 t 11. f. 1, so exactly corresponds with the small barren pimpinelloid fronds of *Lomaria filiformis*, as pointed out by Sir W. Hooker (Sp. Fil vol iii p 34), that it seems to me there must be some error in referring the plant figured by Brackenridge to Viti.

The following species from tropical Polynesia should be recorded here:—1 *Olfersia gorgonea*, Presl, Tent. Pter. p. 235 (*Aconiopteris obtusa*, Fée, Hist Acrost p 80. t. 40 f. 2?), from the Sandwich Islands (D. Nelson! Menzies! Hillebrand! Macrae!). 2 *O Vieillardi*, Carr ms. (*Acrostichum Vieillardi*, Mett Ann Sc Nat. ser. 4. vol. xv p 55), from New Caledonia (Vieillard). A specimen of *Olfersia certina*, Kunze, said to be from the Sandwich Islands (Arch. Menzies) exists in Herb. Mus Brit.

XLIX **Pœcilopteris,** Presl, Tent. Pter. p. 241. Sporangia paginam totam inferiorem frondis fertilis tegentia, in soros superficiales collecta. Venæ irregulariter anastomosantes, venulis ultimis interdum liberis.—Filices rhizomate repente v. scandente, frondibus diplotaxibus simplicibus pinnatis v. bipinnatis.—*Poikilopteris,* Eschw. Linnæa, ii. p. 117. *Hymenodium,* Fée, Hist. Acrost. p. 20. *Neurocallis,* Fée, l. c. p. 19.

In addition to the species described below, the following also occur in tropical Polynesia:—1 *P Smithii,* Carr ms (*Oyrtogonium sinuosum,* J. Sm. Hook. Journ. 1841, p 403, quoad Cuming, n 152), from Aneitum, New Hebrides (M'Gillivray !) 2. *P. Brackenridgei,* Carr ms (*Lomagramma pteroides,* Brack (non Sm.) U. S. Expl Exped *Filices,* p 83), from Tahiti (Nelson !), New Hebrides (C. Moore !), Samoan Islands (U S Expl. Exped.). 3. *P. Requienianum,* Carr. ms (*Acrostichum Requienianum,* Gaudich Voy Freyc. p. 304 t. 4), from Aneitum, New Hebrides (M'Gillivray ! n. 60)

1. **P. Quoyana,** Presl, Epim. Bot. p. 173 (excl. syn.); rhizomate repente, paleaceo; stipitibus semiterctibus, sulcatis, basi dense paleaceis; frondibus membranaceis, glabris, pinnatis, apice attenuatis, sinuato-pinnatifidis, proliferis, fertilibus minoribus, pinnis oblongo-lanccolatis, pinna-tifidis, acuminatis, basi oblique cuneatis; laciniis sterilibus, oblongis, crenato-denticulatis, fertilibus oblongo-lanceolatis, petiolatis.—*Acrostichum Quoyanum,* Gaudich. Voy. Uranie, p 307. pl. 3 *Heteroneuron Quoyanum,* Fée, Hist. Acrost. p. 96 (excl. syn. *Cyrtogonium laciniatum,* J. Smith). *Acrostichum lonchophorum,* Kunze, Fil p. 5. t. 2. *Cyrtogonium palustre,* Brack. U.S. Expl. Exped. *Filices,* p. 86. t. 12.—Viti (Seemann !). Also from Samoan Islands, Tahiti (Banks and Solander ! Barclay ! U. S. Expl. Exped.), Raiatea (Collie !), and Upolu, Navigator's Islands (Sir E. Home !).

2. **P. rivularis,** Carr. ms.; rhizomate repente; stipitibus angularibus, paleaceis; frondibus membranaceis, glabris, oblongis, attenuatis, basi pinnatis, versus apicem sinuato-pinnatifidis, fertilibus minoribus; pinnis integris, oblongo-lanceolatis v. ovatis, obtusis, subfalcatis, apice proliferis.—*Cyrto-gonium rivulare,* Brack. U S Expl. Exped. *Filices,* p. 85. t. 11. f. 2.—Viti, Ovalau, banks of streams, on wet rocks in shady places (U. S. Expl. Exped.).

3. **P. polyphylla,** Carr. ms.; rhizomate scandente, nudo, subquadrangulari, infime radicante; stipitibus sulcatis; frondibus pinnatis v. bipinnatis; pinnis et pinnulis subalternis, subsessilibus, pin-nulis sterilibus, oblongo-lanceolatis, crenato-serratis, sparsim paleaceis, fertilibus stipitatis, lincaribus —*Lomogramma? polyphylla,* Brack. U.S. Expl. Exped. *Filices,* p. 83. t. 12. f. 1. *Chorizopteris bipinnata,* T. Moore, Ind. Fil. p. 257.—Viti (Seemann ! n. 421, 713; Harvey ! U.S. Expl. Exped.) Also from Aneitum, New Hebrides (C. Moore !).

It is probable that *Polybotrya Wilkesiana,* Brack., is only a form of this plant with very narrow pinnules, in which the veining is reduced to a single costal mesh, or perhaps even to free venules. Both fertile and barren fronds, as figured by Brackenridge, agree in every respect with specimens collected by Harvey, except in the venation

The following species should be added here —1. *Hymenodium reticulatum,* T Moore, Ind Fil p. 14, from Sandwich Islands (Strickland ! Hillebrand ! Macrae ! Chamisso, Gaudichaud, etc). 2. *Leptochilus varians,* Mett. Ann Sc Nat ser 4 vol xv. p 56, from New Caledonia (Vieillard)

L. **Hymenolepis,** Kaulf. Enum. Fil. p. 146. t. 1. f. 9. Sporangia costæ imposita, in soros superficiales lineari-elongatos apice frondium collecta. Venæ anastomosantes, areolas irregulares formantes, ultimis venulis liberis.—Filices rhizomate repente, frondibus simplicibus opacis lineari-lanceolatis, apice contracto sporangiferis.—*Macroplethus,* Presl, Epim. Bot p. 141.

1. **H. ophioglossoides,** Kaulf. Enum. Fil. p. 146 (excl. syn); rhizomate repente, paleaceo; stipitibus brevibus, glabris, sulcatis; frondibus elongato- v. angusto-lanceolatis, subcoriaceis, glabris; apice fructifero lineari-obtuso; soris continuis, squamulis obductis.—Viti (Seemann ! n. 726). Also from Aneitum, New Hebrides (M'Gillivray !), and Tahiti (Anderson ! Nelson !).

This species was originally, and has been nearly all along, confounded with Linnæus's *Acrostichum spicatum*, from Bourbon. The primary veins in the Bourbon plants are strong and well marked, while in that from the islands of Eastern Asia and Polynesia the veins are uniform

LI. Chrysodium, Fée, Hist. Acrost. p. 22. Sporangia paginam totam inferiorum pinnarum fiondis fertilis tegentia, in soros superficiales aggregata. Venæ anastomosantes.—Filices rhizomate vix repente, crasso; frondibus monotaxibus pinnatis, pinnis superioribus soriferis.

1. **C. aureum,** Mett. Fil. Lips. p. 21; rhizomate crasso; stipitibus lævibus nudis sulcatis; frondibus pinnatis, rigidis; pinnis sterilibus, lanceolatis v. oblongo-ligulatis, plus minusve angustis, apice acuminatis v. obtusis, margine integris, paululum revolutis; fertilibus angustioribus.—*Acrostichum aureum*, Linn Sp. Pl. p. 1068.—Viti (Seemann! n. 709; Harvey! M'Gillivray! Milne! Sir E. Home!). Also from New Caledonia (Strange!), Tahiti (Banks and Solander!), Raiatea (Collie!), Aneitum, New Hebrides (M'Gillivray!), and Upolu, Navigators' Islands (Sir E. Home!).

Subordo III. OSMUNDACEÆ.

LII. Todea, Willd. Act. Acad Erford. 1802, p. 14. t. 3. f. 1. Sporangia obovato-globosa, pedicellata, dorso annulo obsoleto transversali gibbosa, longitudinaliter dehiscentia, venis simplicibus v. furcatis imposita, in soros oblongos ad venas paginæ inferioris collecta. Venæ simplices v. furcatæ, venulis liberis.—Filices caudice erecto, frondibus coriaceis v. pellucido-membranaceis, bipinnatis, pinnis articulatis.

1. **T. Wilkesiana,** Brack. U. S. Expl Exped. *Filices*, p. 309. t. 43; caudice erecto; stipitibus lævibus, semiteretibus, antice sulcatis; frondibus membranaceis, glabris, bipinnatis; pinnis sessilibus, oblongo-lanceolatis, inferioribus deflexis; rachibus pilosis, alatis; pinnulis oblongis, obtusis, dentatis, basi oblique cuneatis, pellucido-punctatis.—Viti (Seemann! n. 787; M'Gillivray! U. S. Expl. Exped.).

Subordo IV. SCHIZÆACEÆ.

LIII. Schizæa, Smith, Act. Turin. 1790-91, p. 419. Sporangia subsessilia, ovata, annulo apicali completo transverso instructa, pagina inferiori appendicium fertilium pinnæformium adnata. Venæ simplices v. flabellato-dichotomæ, liberæ.—Filices rhizomate repente, frondibus simplicibus v. repetito-dichotomis v. flabellatis.—*Ripidium*, Bernh. Schrad. Journ. 1800, vol. ii. p. 127. *Actinostachys*, Wall. Cat. n. 1.

The following have also been found in tropical Polynesia:—1. *S. fistulosa*, Labill. I'l Nov Holl. vol ii p 103 t 250 f 3, from New Caledonia (Vieillard). 2. *S. bifida*, Willd Sp Pl vol. v. p. 87, from New Caledonia (Vieillard). 3. *S. robusta*, Baker, Syn. Fil. p. 429, from Sandwich Islands (Hillebrand) 4. *S. lævigata*, Mett. Ann. Sc. Nat. ser. 4. vol. xv. p. 85, from New Caledonia (Sinclair! Vieillard), and Isle of Pines (Milne!). 5. *S. intermedia*, Mett l. c. p. 86, from New Caledonia (Vieillard).

1. **S. dichotoma,** Smith, Act. Turin. 1790-91, p 419 (excl. fig.); rhizomate repente, piloso; stipitibus basi semiteretibus, supra sulcatis, submarginatis; frondibus subflabelliformibus, repetitim dichotomis, segmentis linearibus, compressis, coriaceis, medio costatis, plus minusve asperis, apice soriferis; appendicibus soriferis recurvatis, pinnatis; pinnis 10-20 paribus dispositis, oppositis, linearibus, ultime brevioribus.—*Acrostichum dichotomum*, Linn. Sp. Pl. p 1068 (*fide* spec. in Herb. Petiver).—Viti (Harvey! Græffe! Milne! U. S. Expl. Exped.). Also from Samoan Islands (D. Nelson!).

2. **S. Forsteri,** Spreng. Anleit. vol III. p. 175; rhizomate repente; stipitibus basi semiteretibus, antice sulcatis, elongatis; frondibus flabelliformibus, repetitissime dichotomis, segmentis
linearibus compressis coriaceis prominente costatis, glabris v. subscabris, apice soriferis, appendicibus soriferis, brevibus, suberectis, pinnatis; pinnis 3-5 paribus dispositis, oppositis, lineari-
bus, elongatis.—*Schizæa dichotoma,* Forst. (non Linn.) Prodr. n. 415. *Ripidium dichotomum,*
Bernh. Schrad. Journ. 1800, vol. ii. p. 127. t. 2. f. 3. *Schizæa cristata,* Willd. Sp. Pl. vol. v. p 88
S. fastigiata, Smith, Rees Cycl.—Viti (Seemann! n. 792; Harvey! M'Gillivray! U. S. Expl
Exped.). Also from Tahiti (Forster! Banks and Solander! Barclay! n. 3330), Eromanga
(M'Gillivray!), Tonga (Cook!), New Caledonia (Sir E. Home! M'Gillivray!), and Aneitum
(M'Gillivray! Milne! C. Moore!).

3. **S. digitata,** Swartz, Syn. Fil. p 150. t. 4. f. 1; rhizomate repente, paleaceo; frondibus basi
triquetris, supra compressis, longissimis, linearibus, costa postice prominente, glabris; appendicibus
soriferis erectis, nudis, digitatis, dichotomis v. repetito-dichotomis; sporangiis quadriseriatis —
Acrostichum digitatum, Linn. Sp. Pl. p. 1068. *Schizæa digitata,* Swartz, Syn. Fil. p. 150. *Actinostachys digitata,* Wall Cat. n. 1.—Viti (Seemann! n. 793, U. S. Expl. Exped.).

LIV. Hydroglossum, Willd. Sp. Pl. vol. v. p. 77. Sporangia transverse ovalia, lateraliter
medio inserta, vertice annulo multiradiato instructa, in spicis biserialiter disposita, indusiata. Indusium venæ transversæ adnatum, squamæforme, cucullatum, scariosum, persistens. Venæ furcatæ,
venulis reticulatis.—Filices caudice volubili, frondibus palmato-partitis v. pinnatis.—*Lygodictyon,*
J. Smith in Hook. et Bauer Gen. Fil t. 111 B

1 **H. scandens,** Presl, Suppl Tent. Pter p. 373, caudice semitereti; frondibus herbaceis,
pinnatis; pinnis sterilibus, oblongo-lanceolatis, obtusis, inæqualiter cuneatis, fertilibus ovatis,
obtusis, basi truncatis; spicis semiteretibus, subpedicellatis, glaberrimis.—*Ophioglossum scandens,*
Forst. Prodr. n. 412 (non Linn). *Hymenoglossum polycarpum,* Willd. Sp Pl. vol. v. p 79 *Lygo-
dium reticulatum,* Schk. Fil p. 139. *Lygodictyon Forsteri,* J. Sm in Hook. et Bauer Gen. Fil.
t 111 B—Viti (Seemann! n. 790; Harvey! Sir E. Home! Milne! Græffe!) Also from Tahiti
(Cook! Banks and Solander! Barclay! n. 3328; Collie! Bennett!), Raiatea (Collie!), Aneitum,
New Hebrides (M'Gillivray!), and New Caledonia (Strange! C. Moore! M'Gillivray!).

SUBORDO V. MARATTIACEÆ.

LV. Angiopteris, Hoffmann, Comm. Soc. Reg Gott. vol. XII. p. 29. t. 5. Sporangia ovata,
basi subtus affixa, interne rima lineari-elliptica v. obovata dehiscentia, biserialia, in soros lineari-
oblongos aggregata. Indusium inferum, lineare, scariosum, fimbriatum, persistens. Venæ simplices
v furcatæ, liberæ —Filices rhizomate crasso subgloboso, pulvinis frondium lapsarum spiraliter dispositis, frondibus amplis, bipinnatis, pinnulis articulatis.

The following species have been distinguished as found in tropical Polynesia, but the characters given
for their separation do not seem to me, with the materials I have examined, to be sufficient for specific
distinction.—1. *A. evecta,* Hoffm. l c. p 29, from Society Islands (Forster!) and Tahiti (Cook! Banks!)
Allied to *A. evecta.* 2. *A. Durvilleana,* De Vriese, Monogr Maratt. p. 17, from Tahiti (Durville). 3. *A.
longifolia,* Grev. and Hook. Bot. Misc. vol. III p 227, from Society Islands (Matthews, n 2). 4. *A acro-
carpa,* De Vriese, Monogr. Maratt p. 20, from Society Islands (Bidwill) 5. *A. cupreata,* De Vriese, l c
p. 21, from Society Islands (Bidwill). 6. *A. Lasequeana,* De Vriese, l c. p. 25, from Huahine (Nightingale).
And allied to *A commutata,* 7. *A. Brongniartiana,* De Vriese, l. c. p. 30, from Tahiti (*fide* De Vriese).

1. **A. commutata,** Presl, Suppl. Tent. Pter. p. 285; frondibus bipinnatis; pinnis petiolatis,

oblongis, pinnulis petiolulatis linearibus angustato-acuminatis crenatis, basi rotundatis, subtus paleis minutis hinc inde adspersis, acumine acute serrulatis; venis furcatis v. simplicibus; venulis secundariis e sinu crenæ decurrentibus nullis aut obscuris; soris lineari-ellipticis, contiguis, infra marginalibus.—*A. erecta*, Brack. U. S. Expl. Exped. *Filices*, p. 310.—Viti (Seemann! n. 789; Milne! Græffe! U. S. Expl. Exped.). Also from Aneitum, New Hebrides (M'Gillivray!), and Tahiti (Nelson! Barclay! n. 3334).

LVI. **Gymnotheca**, Presl, Suppl. Tent. Pter. in Abhandl. Bohm. Gesellsch. ser. 5. vol. iv. p. 272. Sporangia biseriata, interne rima lineari-elliptica dehiscentia, in soros sessiles oblongos thecæformes bivalvos absque indusio connata. Venæ simplices v. furcatæ, liberæ.—Filices rhizomate crasso globoso, basin squamæformia stipitum gerente; frondium amplis, bipinnatis, pinnulis articulatis.—*Stibasia*, Presl, l. c. 275.

1. **G. Douglassii**, T. Moore, Ind. Fil. p. 121; stipitibus crassis, supra canaliculatis; frondibus ovatis, glaberrimis, bipinnatis; pinnis alternis, linearibus, acutis, pinnulis sessilibus articulatis, oblongo-lanceolatis, serratis, coriaceis; soris oblongis, inframarginalibus.—*Stibasia Douglassii* Presl, l. c. p. 276. *Marattia Douglasii*, Baker, Syn. Fil. p. 441.

LVII. **Marattia**, Swartz, Nov. Gen et Sp. Pl. p. 128. Sporangia biseriata, interne rima lineari dehiscentia, in soros indusiatos sessiles oblongos thecæformes bivalvos connata. Venæ simplices v. furcatæ, liberæ. Indusium lineari-ellipticum v. ovale, scariosum, fimbriatum, persistens.—Filices rhizomate crasso globoso v. caudiciforme, basin squamiformia stipitum gerente; frondibus amplis, bi-tripinnatis, pinnulis articulatis —*Myriotheca*, Commers. in Juss. Gen. Pl. p. 15.

The following species has also been found in tropical Polynesia.—*M attenuata*, Labill. Sert. Austro-Caled p 9 t 13, 14 From New Caledonia (Labillardière, Vieillard) Also from Aneitum, New Hebrides (M'Gillivray!).

1. **M. sorbifolia**, Swartz, Syn. Fil. p. 168; frondibus bipinnatis; pinnis alternis, pinnulis sessilibus, alternis v. suboppositis, lanceolatis, acuminatis, margine subintegris v. serratis, apicem versus serratis, acumine grosse serratis; venis simplicibus v. furcatis; soris oblongis, a margine distantibus —*Myriotheca sorbifolia*, Bory, Voy. vol. i. p 267.—Viti (Seemann! n. 788; Milne!). Also from Aneitum (M'Gillivray! C. Moore!) and New Caledonia (M'Gillivray!).

Subordo VI. OPHIOGLOSSACEÆ.

The following species of this Suborder occur in tropical Polynesia —1. *Botrychium subbifoliatum*, Brack. U.S Expl. Exped. *Filices*, p. 317. t 44 f. 2, from Sandwich Islands (Nelson! Macrae! U. S. Expl. Exped) 2 *Helminthostachys Zeylanica*, Hook. Gen Fil t. 47, from New Caledonia (M'Gillivray! Vieillard)

LVIII. **Ophioglossum**, Linn. Syst. Nat. ed. 1. Sporangia biseriata, margine spicæ compressæ adnata, horizontalia, connata, globosa, in valvas duas æquales hemisphæricas dehiscentia. Spica fructifera frondi opposita, linearis, pedunculata, mucronata. Venæ reticulatæ.—Filices rhizomate subgloboso, frondibus subcarnosis sterilibus simplicibus v. furcatis.—*Ophioderma*, Endl. Gen. Pl. p. 66. *Rhizoglossum*, Presl, Suppl. Tent. Pter. p. 307. *Cheiroglossa*, Presl, l. c. p. 316.

Besides the species described, the following have been found in tropical Polynesia.—1. *O. ellipticum* Hook and Grev Ic. Fil. t 40 A, from the Sandwich Islands (U. S Expl. Exped). 2 *O. concinnum*, Brack. U. S. Expl Exped. *Filices*, p. 315. t. 44 f 1, from Sandwich Islands (U. S. Expl. Exped). 3. *O reticulatum*, Linn. Sp. Pl. p. 1063, from Samoa (U S. Expl Exped).

1. **O. pendulum,** Linn. Sp. Pl. ed. 2. p. 1518; rhizomate subgloboso; frondibus sessilibus, solitariis v. fasciculatis, fasciæformibus, planis, carnosulis, indivisis v. sæpius versus apicem dichotome divisis, basi longissima angustatis; spica fructifera, in parte inferiore frondis obveniente solitaria rarissime gemina, lineari, obtusa.—*Ophioderma pendula,* Endl Gen. Pl. p. 66.—Viti (Seemann! n. 794, Harvey! Milne! Græffe!). Also from Aneitum, New Hebrides (M'Gillivray!), Eromanga (M'Gillivray!), Tahiti (Nelson! Barclay! n. 1335), and Oahu (Nelson! Barclay! n. 1233).

ORDO CVIII. **MUSCI.**

(Auctore W. Mitten)

A. **HOMODICTYI.**—*Foliorum areolatio e cellulis homomorphis.*

1. **ARTHRODONTES.**—*Peristomii dentes 16 vel (dentibus per paria coalitis) 8, vel (dentibus usque ad basin fissis) 32, pluries transversim articulati, e cellularum stratis binis compositi.*

* *Folia in plano horizontali, rarius verticali expansa.*

† *Caulis erectus, procumbens vel repens, ex apice vel ex apicibus ramorum elongatorum rarissime abbreviatorum fertilis.*

The following tribes of Polynesian Mosses have not yet been found represented in Viti, viz —

Tribus I. GRIMMIEÆ.—*Folia viridia, brevia, obscura, sæpe hyalino-pilifera, nervo haud dilatato, cellulis basilaribus haud coloratis. Peristomii dentes integri, vel sæpius irregulariter fissi.*

I GRIMMIA, Ehrb Beitr vol 1 p 176 Caules breves vel elongati, dichotomi vel fasciculatim ramosi, sæpe pulvinatim cæspitantes Folia cellulis densis obscuris areolata. Thecæ in pedunculo breviusculo recto vel curvato læves vel plicatæ, æquales, peristomii dentibus 16 solidis vel divisis pertusisvo rarius nullis, calyptris mitriformibus vel dimidiatis. Musci rupestres, ut plurimum cæspites canos formantes.—An extensive genus, of which the greater number of the species are found in the northern hemisphere, and prefer to grow on rocks or stones in very exposed situations.

1. *G ovata,* Web et Mohr, Bryol Europ. t. 17 et 18, monoica, compacte cæspitosa; caulis furcatus, folia erecto-patentia, inferiora apice obtusa, superiora subulato-angustata cano-pilifera, margine uno latere recurvo, nervo percurrente carinata, cellulis basilaribus oblongis, lateralibus paucis rectangulis, superioribus parvis rotundis limitibus pellucidis, perichætialia erecta majora longius incana; pedunculus brevis, rectus, vix vel parum ultra apices foliorum perichætalium productus, theca oblongo-ovalis, lævis, olivaceo-fusca, basi subcallosa, operculo conico-rostrato, peristomii dentibus fissis perforatisve, calyptra lobata —Sandwich Islands (Herb Hooker!).—This species forms compact tufts of a greyish-green colour above from the white points of its leaves; the stems are seldom more than inch in height, and below have the older foliage blackish It is found nearly all over the world.

II. GLYPHOMITRIUM, Brid. Meth p. 30 *Brachysteleum,* Reichenb *Ptychomitrium,* Bruch et Schimp Caules pulvinatim cæspitantes. Folia canaliculata, firma, siccatione crispata, cellulis obscuris Theca in pedunculo recto lævis, rarissime subplicata, peristomii dentibus sæpius inæqualiter divisis; calyptra mitriformis, plicis lævibus vel interdum dentatis

1 *G Mülleri,* Mitt Linn. Soc Journ 1859; caulis humilis, folia a basi lata subquadrata superne paululum dilatata vaginante angustata patentia sublanceolata, apice obtuse acuta subcucullata, nervo subsummo apice evanido carinata, integerrima, cellulis basi ad medium partis latioris oblongis rectangulatis, inde ad apicem usque parvis rotundis, perichætialia tria breviora ovata acuminata; theca in pedunculo 3-4-lineari ovalis, ætate corrugata, operculo subulato subæquilongo, peristomio dentibus divisis vel pertusis, calyptra plicis lævibus —Lord Howe's Island (Milne!).—A little more robust than the South African *G crispatum,* Hook. Bot. Misc 1830, t. 36. This species is found also in Australia, whence it was originally sent by Dr. F von Müller.

Tribus II. TORTULEÆ —*Folia viridia, obscura, cellulis inferioribus haud conspicue diversis. Peristomium simplex, rarius duplex, dentibus sæpe angustis elongatis tortis, interdum nullum.*

I WEISIA, Hedw Fund vol ii p 90 Caulis ex apice fertilis Folia viridia vel flavo-viridia, margine incurva, cellulis parvis obscuris areolata Peristomium si adsit dentibus 8 vel 16, ad basin usque discretis, calyptra dimidiata parva.—*Hyophila,* Brid vol. i. p 760.

1 *W. Samoana*, Mitt. Journ of the Proceed Linn Soc 1868, p. 193 (*Hyophila*), pulvinatim cæspitosa, caulis humilis; folia patentia, a basi brevi contracta ovali-oblonga, apice obtuse acuta, nervo percurrente, margine apice crenulato integerrimo, ad latera folii inflexo, cellulis superioribus minutis rotundatis viridibus, basilibus paucis oblongis pellucidis majoribus.—Samoa, Tutuila, on trees (Powell 123).—More robust than *W. (Hyophila) Javanica*, Nees et Blume, the leaves not so acute, and at their apices more or less distinctly crenulate

II. ENCALYPTA, Schreb. Gen Pl n 1613 Calyptra magna, cylindracea, inflata, rostrata.

1. *E. Sandwichensis*, Sull Amer. Expl. Exped. 1859, p. 6; "monoica, foliis oblongo-lanceolatis et elongato-spathulatis convolutis papillosis evanido-costatis, capsula gymnostoma, cylindracea, sicca 8-10-sulcata, calyptra tota superficie papillosa, flore masculo monophyllo"—Hawaii, sides of Mauna Kea, East Maui, banks of the Crater (Amer. Exped.[1]) —Densely cæspitose, 1 inch high, radiculose, leaves soft, margins crenulate, upper cells hexagonal-rotund. Capsule slightly apophysate.

Tribus III. ORTHOTRICHIEÆ —*Caules erecti, apice fertiles vel repentes ex apicibus ramorum fructiferi Folia viridia, obscura, cellulis inferioribus parum diversis vel elongatis Peristomium simplex vel duplex, interdum nullum; dentibus latis cum processibus internis alternantibus.*

I MACROMITRIUM, Brid. vol. i. p. 306. Caulis repens, ex apicibus ramorum fertilis. Theca lævis plicatave. Peristomium externum dentibus discretis geminatisve, internum processibus totidem, dentibus similibus vel in membranam truncatam coalitis, sæpe autem simplex, vel omnino deest. Calyptra campanulata plicata, basi plurifida.—A very extensive genus of tropical and austral species, all conspicuous for their lobed calyptras.

* *Goniostoma.*—Rami simplices vel fasciculatim ramosi. Folia cellulis inferioribus rectis. Theca ore intensius colorato subcarnoso

Pedunculus abbreviatus.

1. *M. brevisetum* (sp nov.), Mitt.; pusillum; rami breves, erecti, simplices, folia patentia lanceolato-ligulata obtusa nervo in mucronem brevissimum excurrente carinata, margine apicem versus minuto crenulato, cellulis superioribus rotundis obscuris, basilibus paucis oblongis, perichætialia longiora, apice in mucronem piliferum acuminata; theca in pedunculo eam breviore emergens oblongo-ovalis, ad medium usque plicata, operculo subulato, calyptra ramentis sparsis pilosa.—Oahu (Beechey!).—In its short fruit-stalk, this species differs from all that have yet been described.

Pedunculus elongatus

2 *M. prorepens*, Hook. Musc. Exot. t. 120 (*Orthotrichum*), rami breves, graciles, fasciculatim ramosi, in cæspitem congesti; folia erecto-patentia sicca arcte imbricato-contorta lanceolato-ligulata apice obtuse acuta vel brevissime acuminata margine uno latere reflexo integerrima nervo percurrente superne carinata inferne in plica subcomplicata sepulto, cellulis in dimidio folii inferiore erectiore elongatis, papillis grossis, in dimidio superiore minutis rotundis obscuris papillis minoribus, perichætialia interna brevia ovata obtusa, theca in pedunculo brevi ovalis, ore plicata, calyptra ramentis appressis pilosa.—Norfolk Island (F Bauer!), also in New Zealand. This small species appears to be less frequently sent from New Zealand than some of the nearly allied ones, none of which, however, have their leaves in the dry state so closely contorted.

3. *M. piliferum*, Schw. t. 172; rami erecti, humiles, fasciculatim ramosi; folia a basi brevi erectiore patenti-incurva sicca contorta anguste lanceolata lineali-attenuata apice obtusa pilo fulvo terminata nervo percurrente carinata integerrima, cellulis superioribus densis opacis inferioribus pellucidioribus inter se remotiusculis rotundis basilibus paucis oblongis, perichætialia longiora exserta erecto-patentia lanceolato-subulata attenuata, theca in pedunculo breviusculo oblongo-ovalis, fere ad basin usque plicata, fusca, operculo subulato; calyptra ramentis pallide flavis erectis dense vestita.—Sandwich Islands (Douglas! Menzies! Beechey!) The hair-pointed leaf, so obvious in this species, is of rare occurrence in the genus

4 *M. Owahiense*, C. Mueller, Bot Zeit 1861, p. 359; monoicum, late intertexte cæspitosum, humile, gracillimum, longe prorepens, ramulis pinnatim dispositis brevissimis gracillimis sterilibus sensim minoribus instructum, unde in stolonem elongatum radicantem secundifolium protractum, ramuli fertiles ante stolonem illum egredientes, breves, apice fastigiatim divisi, virentes, dein lutei vel sordide fuscescentes, majore haud turgescentes sed graciles, folia crispatula humore erecto-patula apice incurva multo minora angustiora lanceolata breviter acuminata nervo excurrente acuta nec pungentia profunde carinata ad nervum basilarem ferrugineum parum latius concava, margine erecto deplanato vel reflexo integerrima, e cellulis lævibus diaphanis apice quadratis mox longioribus pariter incrassatis basi elongatis luteis vel aureis areolata, perichætialia multo minora non cuspidem exsertum sistentia late lanceolata, intima nervo longius protracto tenuiter cuspidata; theca in pedunculo elongato flexili rubente lævi erecta, angustissime cylindrico-oblonga, parva, distincte sexies sulcata, nec ore plicata, nec sub orificio ventricose turgescens, peristomio longe infra

orificium constrictum oriundo simplici, e dentibus lanceolatis pallidis asperulis brevibus siccitate immerso-incurvis composito, calyptra nuda fusca lævi.—*M. Reinwardti*, Sull. Amer. Expl Exp p 7, huc forsan revocandum.—Oahu (Didrichsen!), ad montem Kaah (Macrae!); Sandwich and Society Islands (Amer Expl Exp). *M. Reinwardti* quasi dimmutivum, sed primo visu gracilitate omnium partium magna distans, cæteris notis supra dictis differre videtur—Macrae's specimen with the single capsule, which is not, however, very evidently plicate, appears to belong to this species

5 *M angulatum*, Mitt Linn Soc Journ. 1868, p 167, rami humiles, graciles, ramosi, laxe cæspitosi, folia patentia pentasticha sicca appressa contorta oblongo-linearia acuta nervo percurrente carinata, marginibus cellulis prominulis crenulatis, cellulis omnibus grossiusculis rotundatis obscuris, perichætialia propria nulla, vaginula pilosa, theca in pedunculo brevi tetragono asperrimo ovata, ore parvo demum quater plicato operculo subulato, calyptra ramentis inferioribus divaricatis pilosa—Samoa Islands, Tutuila on Hibiscus trees (1000 ft), (Powell! 67)—Very nearly resembling *M orthostichum*, Nees ab E, from Java, but with leaves not wider at their base, and patent, not squarrose or divaricated.

** *Leiostoma.*—Theca ore lævi haud plicata   Folia cellulis inferioribus rectis.

6 *M Tongense*, Sull. Amer Expl Exp p. 7. t. 5, rami abbreviati, pusilli; folia densa patentia sicca contorta crispata auguste lanceolato-ligulata obtusa cum apiculo brevissimo nervo percurrente carinata, cellulis superioribus parvis rotundis infra folii medium parietibus pellucidis distinctis basilibus angustis elongatis, perichætialia conformia, theca in pedunculo foliis perichætialibus breviore oblonga, lævis, sicca infra os rufum contracta, operculo subulato, peristomium dentibus brevibus pallidis, calyptra pallida, ad basin thecæ descendens, pilis sparsis obtecta—Tongatabu, Friendly Islands (American Exp!), Lord Howe's Island (M'Gillivray!), Isle of Pines (Strange!).   A small species growing in thin matted patches, it is allied to *M involutifolium*, Hook et Grev, from Australia

*** *Campylodictyon.*—Folia cellulis inferioribus curvatis.   Theca lævis—This group consists of a considerable number of species, nearly all confined to the Eastern Archipelago

7 *M incurvifolium*, Hook et Grev (*Orthotrichum*), rami elongati, simplices vel ramosi; folia patentia apicibus incurvis erectis lanceolato-lineali ligulata apice obtuse acuminata, nervo carinata integerrima, cellulis superioribus minutis rotundis obscuris inferioribus minus obscuris basilibus oblongis haud lunato-curvulis, perichætialia acutiora cæterum caulinis similia; theca in pedunculo brevi globoso-ovata, lævis, operculo subulato, calyptra pilis brevibus erectis inspersa—Tahiti (Menzies!), Pacific Islands (Beechey! Nightingale!), Pitcairn's Island (Beechey!)

8. *M. Powellii*, Mitt Linn. Soc Journ. 1868, p 168, rami elongati, in cæspitibus latis aggregati, folia dense inserta a basi brevi erecta recurva divaricata lineali-lanceolata sensim ad apicem acutum angustata nervo rufescente subexcurrente carinata integerrima, cellulis basilibus elongatis pellucidis subrectis dimidium folii longitudinis occupantibus sensim in rotundatas obscuriusculas transeuntibus, perichætialia interna breviora lanceolato-subulata pellucida, vaginula pilis paucis brevibus, theca in pedunculo breviusculo, parva, ovalis, ore parvo, operculo subulato, peristomio dentibus brevibus pallidis, calyptra ramentis appressis pilosa.—Samoan Islands, Tutuila, on Cocoa-nut trees near the sea-level (Powell! n. 110).—This species nearly resembles *M incurvifolium*, but differs in its gradually narrowed acute leaves.

9. *M. Beecheyanum*, Mitt Linn. Soc Journ 1868, p 167, rami elongati, cæspitosi; folia dense inserta a basi brevi erectiore recurva patentia apicibus incurvis a media sensim subloriformi-angustata, apice obtusiuscula subacuta, nervo pellucidiore in carina profunde exarata percurrente, integerrima, cellulis inferioribus curvatis pellucidis usque ad tertiam partem folii longitudinis productis, inde parvis rotundatis obscuriusculis, perichætialia breviora erecta pellucidiora, vaginula ramentis exsertis pilosa, theca in pedunculo brevi ovalis, operculo longe subulato, ore parvo ætate obtuse plicato gymnostoma; calyptra ramentosa.—Samoan Islands, Tutuila, on living trees, mostly *Hibiscus tiliaceus*, 20–500 ft. (Powell! n 1).

10 *M glaucum*, Mitt Linn. Soc. Journ. 1868, p. 167; rami elongati, ramulosi, late cæspitosi; folia quinquefaria dense inserta in spiras ad dextram ascendentes disposita elongate lanceolata apice obtusa, nervo in mucronem excurrente, dimidio folii inferiore erectiore, superiore recurvo divaricato carinato, apice subcucullato-carinata integerrima, cellulis inferioribus pellucidis arcuatis ad nervum ultra folii medium productis, superioribus minutis rotundatis obscuris, perichætialia plura conformia æquilonga erecta pellucida; theca in pedunculo breviusculo, ovata, ore parvo operculo subulato; peristomium parvum, dentibus brevibus pallidis; calyptra ramentis appressis eam longitudine haud excedentibus pilosa—Samoa Islands, Tutuila, forming extensive mats on Breadfruit-trees nearly at the sea-level (Powell! 109)—Like *M. gracile* in habit, but with leaves having a longer pale base, their apices complicate, so as to appear more acute than they are in reality.

II. CRYPTOCARPUS, Dozy et Molk Musc Frond Archip Ind p 37. t 15.   Caulis repens, radicans, ramos breves erectos exinde in prolongationibus propriis diversifoliis apice fertilibus eductis fovens   Theca immersa, gymnostoma. Calyptra parva, mitriformis —A remarkable genus, in its foliage and habit, before the fertile prolongations are produced, exactly corresponding with *Macromitrium*, but in the production of special short-leaved shoots, on which the fruit is borne, analogous only to those species of *Campylopus*, like *C crasperatus*, which are referable to the subgenus or group *Thysanomitrium*.

1. *C. cymosus* (sp nov.), Mitt.; caulis radicans, foliis sursum curvatis appressis lanceolatis; rami erecti, humiles, in cæspitem congesti, foliis patenti-incurvis ligulatis obtusis, nervo in mucronem excurrente, margine basin versus papillis elongatis setiformibus ciliatis, cellulis superioribus rotundis obscuris inferioribus angustis pellucidioribus, subito in tertilibus, in foliis abbreviatis, quinquefariis imbricatis e basi erecta patenti-recurvis late ovatis obtusis, nervo flavo in mucronem excurrente, margine basi crenulata mutatis; folia perichætialia erecta, oblonga, obtusa, inferne cellulis angustis pellucidis areolata, theca ovata, ore nigro-fusco nitido; ramus fructifer intra perichætium innovans, interdum subcymoso-divisus —Isle of Pines, on stones on the main peak (Milne !). Barren branches about two lines high, the fertile prolongations from half to three-quarters of an inch high, simple or much divided at the top. The apices of the perichætial leaves are about equal with the mouth of the capsule. This appears to differ from the *C. apiculatus*, Dozy et Molk. Musc Archip Ind t. 15, in the following particulars.—the leaves of the barren shoots, or those of the base of the fertile ones, are much narrower, not more than half the width in proportion to their length, and from this cause are not imbricated, as represented in the plate at figs 3 and 4; in the foliage of the fertile prolongations and the perichætium there appears to be no difference. *C. brachiatus*, Hook et Wils. Icon. Plant. Rar. t 746 B (*Macromitrium*), differs in the same respects from *C. apiculatus*, the leaves being very much narrower, and without the ciliiform papillæ at their base. Another specimen sent from Kalangan, Borneo, by Motley, differs in habit, and in the foliage of its fertile prolongations being more lax and curved.

Tribus IV. FUNARIÆ.—*Peristomium internum, plus minus evolutum, processibus planis vel nullis. Calyptra sæpe inflata, rostro tubuloso*

I. FUNARIA, Schreb. Theca inæqualis, lævis vel plicata. Peristomium externum dentibus 16 obliquis apicibus cohærentibus, internum laciniis teneris dentibus oppositis.

1. *F. hygrometrica*, Hedw. Fund vol i. t. 5. f. 12; caulis brevis; folia comalia incurvo-imbricata, concava, ovali-acuminata, integerrima, nervo brevissime excurrente, cellulis laxis lævibus rhombeo-hexagonis areolata; theca in pedunculo elongato humido curvato sicca recto horizontalis, pyriformis, ore magno obliquo deorsum spectante, operculo convexo, peristomio completo; flos masculus in ramo brevi, foliis subserrulatis —Isle of Pines, in burnt places (Milne !). The specimens of this cosmopolite species differ in no particular from the usual European state.

Tribus V. BARTRAMIÆ —*Theca ut plurimum globosa plicataque. Peristomii interni processus carinati, per carinam fissi. Folia limitibus cellularum prominulis papillosa*

I BARTRAMIA, Hedw. Musc. Frond. Caulis erectus, dichotomus vel ramis infra florem egredientibus verticillatim ramosus. Folia pellucida vel obscura. All the Polynesian species yet known belong to the natural group which was designated by Bridel *Philonotis*; these differ in habit from the group of species with thickened dark green foliage, and which are considered *Eubartramiæ*. In *Philonotis* the stems are usually slender, and are branched with a number of equal innovations, arising from just below the inflorescence in a verticillate manner. The leaves are small and usually nearly pellucid, with narrow nerves, the areolation composed of cells which have their upper extremities prominent, and in many species on account of this peculiarity, and the margin of the leaf being recurved, their leaves appear more serrate than they really are.

1. *B. asperifolia*, Mitt Linn Soc Journ. vol x. p 185; dioica; caules humiles, graciles, in cæspites latos aggregati, folia patentia ovato-lanceolata, ramea oblongo-lanceolata, omnia nervis dorso superne serratis percurrentibus, marginibus anguste recurvis serrulatis, cellulis pellucidis, superioribus oblongis, inferioribus subquadratis, perichætialia longiora a basi latiora subulata serrulata, theca in pedunculo elongato, subglobosa, inæqualis, horizontalis, plicata, operculo depresse conico; peristomium depressum, internum externumque dentibus fere lævibus, flos masculus parvus, foliis a basi rotundata subulatis erectis —Samoa, Tutuila, on damp earth and on rocks by watercourses, 20–100 ft (Powell ! n. 28). A small pale green species, with stems from a quarter to half an inch high, with small short and rough leaves from the prominence of the serrature of the margins and nerves.

2. *B obtusifolia* (sp. nov), cæspitosa; caulis crassiusculus, ruber; folia glauco-viridissima, erecto-patentia, incurva, laxe imbricata, ovato-oblonga, obtusa, concava, nervo infra apicem evanido, dorso cellulis prominulis subdentato, margine fere ad apicem usque anguste reflexo subcrenulata, apice erecta, cellulis laxissimis ovali-hexagonis pellucidis areolata.—Ysabel (Veitch! in Herb. Hooker). A small species with stems, in the imperfect state in which it was gathered, about half an inch high; distinct from the Javan *B. laxissima*, C Mueller, in its obtuse leaves. Another species was gathered in Hawaii by Menzies.

Tribus VI BRYEÆ.—*Theca ut plurimum clavata, lævis.   Peristomii interni processus carinati, integri vel rarissime divisi.   Folia lævia.   Calyptra dimidiata.*

* Flores in caule primario vel in innovationibus terminales

† Folia undique inserta.

I LEPTOSTOMUM, R. Brown, Linn. Soc Trans. vol x. p. 130.   Peristomium simplex, internum, membrana indivisa.

1. *L macrocarpum*, Hedw. Musc Frond vol. ii t. 10 (*Bryum*), caules inferne tomento rufo intertexti, folia patentia, oblongo-spathulata, obtusa, carinato-concava, margine superno revoluta, integerrima, nervo in pilum brevem simplicem vel elongatum ramosum excurrente, cellulis hexagonis parietibus angustis utriculo anguloso contracto repletis; perichætialia conformia, margine latius revoluta, nervo longius excurrente, magis ramoso, theca in pedunculo elongato ovali-elliptica, erecta, operculo parvo conico-hemisphærico.—Tahiti (Banks and Solander!), Norfolk Island (Allan Cunningham! Herb Hooker)—Specimens smaller than those from New Zealand.   All the species of this genus in the large size of their capsules, and in their general appearance, correspond with *Bryum*, but differ in the firm and dense areolation of their leaves. The genus is peculiar to the islands of the Pacific Ocean, including Australia, Tasmania, and New Zealand, and the western and extreme southern shores of S. America

II BRYUM, Linn.   Peristomium duplex, internum sæpius perfectum, rarius imperfectum—A very extensive genus, all the species of which are generally conspicuous for the large size of their elliptical pyriform or clavate, erect or more frequently pendulous capsules   A great difference exists among the species in the size and substance of the leaves, but they appear to be so intimately connected by intermediate states that it is difficult to define groups which, at first sight, appear sufficiently remote to form natural sections.

* *Dicranobryum*, C Mueller, Syn. vol. i. p 309 —Theca erecta inclinatave.   Peristomium internum incompletum.

1. *B coarctatum*, C. Mueller, Syn vol i. p.312; Dozy et Molk Bryol Javan t 115; synoicum; caulis humilis, folia comalia parva, ovato-lanceolata, acuminata, nervo crassiusculo rufo excurrente, margine integerrima inferne recurva, cellulis parvis oblongis, pedunculus elongatus; theca oblonga, inclinata vel erecta, collo lævi vel tuberculis prominulis distorto, operculo conico acuminato, annulo magno, peristomio externo dentibus angustis, interno processibus abbreviatis angustis in membrana alte exserta imposita, ciliis nullis.—Friendly Islands, Vavau and Lefuka (Harvey!), Samoa, Tutuila, on stones and walls (Powell! n. 16)—This species was first described as dioicous, and is also so described and figured in the 'Bryologia Javanica' above referred to, but Javan specimens from Junghuhn have the antheridia present in the fertile flower in the same manner as in the specimens from Polynesia; some European species which have synoicous fertile flowers produce also male flowers only on branches arising from the same stem   The affinity of this small species is with *B. atropurpureum*, Web. et Mohr, and with this it accords in the colour of its foliage and fruit, as well as in having the neck of the capsule distorted; but in the defective internal peristome it agrees with some Indian and tropical American species.   All these species differ from those of the group which has been named *Brachymenium*, in being always found growing on the earth, and not on the bark of trees.

** *Webera*, Hedw.—Theca inclinata pendulave   Peristomium internum processibus ciliisque plus minus perfectis   Folia nitida, immarginata.

2 *B nutans*, Hedw. Musc Frond vol i t 4, synoicum; caulis humilis, folia inferiora patentia lanceolata, nervo sub apice evanido, margine superno serrulata, cellulis ubique æqualibus elongatis, comalia duplo longiora lineali-lanceolata, interiora minora angustiora argutius serrulata, nervis percurrentibus; pedunculus elongatus; theca nutans vel pendula, sporangio breviter ovali, collo subæquilongo, sicca crassiusculo corrugato subplicato, operculo convexo acuto, peristomium breviusculum, internum ciliis cohærentibus—St Paul's Island (Milne!); Isle of Pines (Strange!)—These specimens appear to possess no difference in aspect, size, or structure from the usual European form

*** *Eccremothecium*, Mitt. Linn. Soc. Journ. 1868.—Theca inclinata pendulave   Peristomium internum processibus ciliisque sæpius perfectis   Folia rarius nitida, sæpius limbo marginata

3. *B megalostegium*, Sull. Amer. Expl Exped 1859, p. 9. t 7.; dioicum, dense cæspitosum, foliis ovato-lanceolatis, costa excurrente breviter cuspidatis, marginibus integerrimis planis; capsula clavata, pyriformi-incurva, nutante vel pendula, late annulata, pachydermi macrostoma; operculo permagno, subhemisphærico, apiculato.—Hawaii, forests on the sides of Mauna Loa (American Expedition!); Raoul Island,

Kermandee Islands (M'Gillivray!); Samoa, Tutuila (Powell!)—Compared by the author to *B. pallens*, Sw, and *B. turbinatum*, Hedw, and described as from 1–2 inches high, but the figure represents it from half an inch to an inch high. The specimens from the Kermandee Islands are shorter even than this, but correspond very well in the form of the leaves. It seems to be a small species allied to the European *B. erythrocarpum*, Schw., and the *B chrysoneuron*, C Muller, so frequent in New Zealand.

4 *B Billardieri*, Schw t 76; " caule mediocri bifido, foliis oblongis obliquo cuspidatis immarginatis dentatis, theca pendula incurva "—New Belgium (Labillardière!); Lord Howe's Island (Milne!)—" Caulis primarius semiuncialis, pone florem ramos aliquot simplices edens, semiunciales aut unciales; folia densa et in rosulam congesta in caule primario et ad apices ramorum, sparsa in inferiore ramorum parte; folia concava, carinata, patula, oblonga, apice dentata, sæpe obliqua, absque margine notabili, siccitate undulata et paululum complicata, amœne viridia, nervus crassus, ferrugineus, ex apice folii emergit absque comitante parenchymate et recurvatur, quindecies ibi brevior est quam folium, areolæ reticuli e rhomboideo subrotundi; seta sesquiuncialis aut biuncialis, apice ad horizontem curvata; theca oblonga, incurva, et per curvaturam suam pendula, ore vix contracta, ut seta operculum et peristomium externum e fusco brunnea, operculum plano-convexum, mucronulatum."—The specimens collected by Milne consist of only a few incomplete stems, but seem to agree with the figure and the above description given by Schwægrichen It is probable that the *B. rufescens*, Hook. f et Wils. Fl. Tasmanica, p. 192. t. 171 f 1, belongs to this species, for it corresponds with the description and figure in the form and margin of its leaves, as well as in the nerve being excurrent into a terete point.

5. *B. leptothecium*, Tayl in Phytologist, 1811, p 1094; caulis gracilis, folia in rosulis congesta, patentia, oblongo-obovata vel spathulata, nervo apice cum limbo marginali coalito in mucronem brevem recurvum producto; cellulis superioribus oblongo-hexagonis, utriculo contracto repletis, limitibus angustis marginalibus angustis in seriebus pluribus congestis limbum tenerum denticulatum sistentibus; theca in pedunculo elongato sporangio cylindraceo subrecto, collo sensim angustato curvato pendula, operculo depresso-conico —Society Islands, barren (Bidwill! in Herb Hooker).—Stems nearly an inch high, and to all appearance not different from the states so frequent in Australia and Tasmania

6 *B. Commersoni*, Brid. Mant p. 119, Schw t. 80; caulis plus minus elongatus, laxe cæspitosus, folia ubique per caulis longitudinem æqualia vel in rosulis congesta patula obovato-spathulata acuminata, nervo breviter excurrente mucronata margine inferne integerrima e medio usque ad apicem denticulis brevibus serrata, cellulis hexagono-ovalibus chlorophyllosis, parietibus mollibus, marginalibus longioribus limbum indistinctum formantibus, perichætialia interna minora; theca in pedunculo elongato horizontalis, elongato-cylindracea, arcuata, operculo conico acuto —Lord Howe's Island, low ground abundant, but barren (Milne! Herb. Hooker, 47).—Specimens small and short, but agreeing in the dull, dark green colour of the younger and pale fulvous tint of the older leaves, as well as in the areolation and margin with *B Beyrichianum*, Hornsch., and *B. umbraculum*, Burchell, Hook. Musc. Exot. t. 133, between all which the correspondence is so close as to lead to the supposition they may be states of only one widely spread species.

III CRYPTOPODIUM, Brid vol ii p 30. Caulis erectus Folia undique æqualia, angusta, e cellulis parvis firmis areolata Theca in pedunculo brevi lævis. Peristomium completum

1. *C Bartramioides*, Hook. Musc. Exot. t. 18 (*Bryum*), caulis simplex vel innovationibus ramosus, folia inferiora parva appressa sensim superne longitudine increscentia, superiora patentia vel subsecunda a basi suboblonga sensim subulato angustata rigida setacea, nervo marginibusque supra basin oblongam usque ad apicem dentibus brevibus geminatis serratis, cellulis firmis rotundis parvis inferioribus suboblongis, perichætialia a basi latiora lanceolata subulata caulinis similia thecam ovalem inclinatam longe superantia; pedunculus vix theca longior; peristomium dentibus lineali-subulatis firmis, internum processibus carinatis parce pertusis, ciliisque tribus æquilongis interpositis in membrana usque ad dentium medium exserta impositis.—Sandwich Islands (Gaudichaud!)—A remarkable Moss, having the rigid stems and foliage of *Rhizogonium spiniforme*, but with its fruit terminal, and not exserted beyond the leaves It is not allied to *Bartramia*.

†† Folia tristicha, dimorpha.

IV. CALOMNION, Hook f et Wils. Theca erecta, gymnostoma

1. *C denticulatum*, Mitt Linn Soc. Journ. vol. x p 192; folia lateralia omnia superficiebus superioribus ad idem latus spectantia, patentia, oblonga, nervo in mucronem excurrente, margine a medio ad apicem usque denticulata; folia media appressa, dimidio breviora, suborbiculata, superne dentata; folia omnia cellulis parvis rotundatis interstitiisque pellucidis firmis, perichætialia longiora spathulata lineari-lanceolataque; theca in pedunculo gracili, ovalis, erecta, operculo subulato. Planta mascula flore apicali gemmiformi —Samoa, Upolu, on trees (Powell! n. 103)—Corresponding in size, habit, and appearance with *C. lætum*, Hook. f. et Wils Fl. New Zealand, pl. 87. f 5, but with denticulate leaves, and the capsule appears to have a smaller mouth The stem is said in the 'Handbook of the Flora of New Zealand' to be creeping, but this is not observable in the specimens of the Samoan species.

††† Folia tetrasticha.

V. DREPANOPHYLLUM, Rich in Hook Musc Exot. Folia bifarie compressa, falciformi-curvata, plana.

1. *D semilimbatum*, Mitt Linn Soc Journ vol x. p. 194 t. 5. E; caules in cæspitem aggregati, dichotome divisi, erecti?; folia distiche compressa, nervo rufo in mucronem brevissimum excurrente, lamina folii latere superiore (*i e* caulis apicem versus) ambitu semiorbiculari, limbo cartilagineo incrassato rufo superne subcrenulato integerrimove, fere ad apicem usque continuo marginata, lamina latere inferiore multo angustiore immarginata, apice subcrenata, basin versus angustata et decurrente (ambitu igitur folii ovali-oblongo acuto, nervo uno latere propinquiore) ; cellulæ quadratæ rotundatæque, firmæ, pellucidæ, læves , folia perichætialia magis oblonga, acutiora, cæterum caulinis similia —Samoa, Tutuila (Powell! n. 135) — Very much smaller than the Equatorial American *D fulvum*, Rich ; but, so far as can be judged from the specimens without fruit, closely allied and, in all probability, congeneric with it.

** Flores in ramulo brevissimo basilari.

VI. RHIZOGONIUM, Brid vol. ii. p 661 Caules erecti, subsimplices, rarius ramosi. Folia undique æqualia vel compressa, versus apices caulium decrescentia. Theca longe pedunculata, peristomio perfecto

* *Pyrrhobryum*, Mitt Linn Soc Journ vol. x.—Folia undique inserta, rigida, cellulis densis rotundis areolata Theca plicata

1 *R spiniforme*, L. (*Hypnum*) , folia angustissime lineari-lanceolata, nervo percurrente, dorso dentato, margine duplicato-serrata, perichætialia ovato-subulata simpliciter serrulata , theca oblonga, operculo brevirostro, peristomio interno processibus quam dentes brevioribus in membrana fere ad eorum medium exserta impositis, ciliis obsoletis —Samoa, Upolu, on trees (1000–2000 feet) (Powell ! n 90), Sandwich Islands (Douglas ! n 60) —Possibly distinct from the widely-distributed *P. spiniforme*, so common in tropical America.

2 *R pungens*, Sull. Proceed. Amer. Acad of Arts and Sc. vol. iii. ; dioicum , cæspite denso hispido e viridi spadiceo ; caulibus bi-triuncialibus basi fructiferis erectiusculis simplicibus inferne tomento atropurpureo dense vestitis , foliis laxiusculo dispositis patenti-divergentibus carinato-concavis semiuncialibus (arista inclusa) strictiusculis rigidis pungentibus elliptico-lanceolatis, costa valida subtereti in aristam dorso et lateribus grosse dentatam lamina quintuplo longiorem excurrente instructis, basi valde incrassatis, e cellulis minutis densis subquadratis compositis, margine duplicato-dentato vel potius bilamelloso, lamellis dentatis perichætiis radicalibus brevissime stipitatis ; foliis perichætialibus exterioribus lanceolatis dentatis, interioribus oblongis integerrimis, omnibus laxius reticulatis basi vaginantibus costa excurrente valida dentata longissime aristatis ; archegoniis longiusculis numerosis (10–50) copiose paraphysatis, paraphysibus 7–10-septatis archegonia paululum superantibus —Sull l. c —Hawaii district of Puna on the south-west coast (Amer. Exped) —This must be considerably larger than any other species yet known.

3 *R setosum*, Mitt Journ of the Proceed Linn Soc. 1868, p 174 ; dioicum ; folia in ramis sterilibus patentia, recta subsecundave, apicalia erecta appressa, a basi sensim subulato-angustata, elongata, setacea, rigida, nervo crasso percurrente, superne dorso dentato, margine incrassata, basi integerrima superne breviter duplicato-dentata, a medio usque ad apicem dentibus validioribus simplicibus serrata, cellulis parvis rotundis limitibus latis ; perichætium in ramo brevi, foliis a basi parva ovata longe anguste subulata curvata, nervo excurrente marginibusque superne dentatis Habitus *R spiniformis*.—Samoa, Upolu, on trees on the way to Lanutoo, 2000 ft. (Powell ! n 11). In size, mode of growth, and in the colour of its foliage, like *P spiniforme*, but with leaves scarcely half as wide, more bristle-like and rigid , the teeth towards the apex of the leaf are evidently a continuation of the margin, so that the nerve is not terete and excurrent as is said to be the case in *P. pungens*, which must also be a much larger Moss.

** *Photinophyllum*, Mitt Linn. Soc Journ vol x —Folia undique inserta, cellulis majusculis pellucidis areolata. Theca lævis

4 *R. subbasilare*, Hook Musc Exot t. 10 (*Hypnum*) , caulis erectus , folia patentia oblongo-lanceolata planiuscula nervo infra apicem evanido, marginibus superioribus, denticulis simplicibus serratis, cellulis oblongis pellucidis parietibus angustissimis, perichætialia lanceolata acuminata ; theca in pedunculo elongato cylindracea, horizontalis nutansve, operculo conico.—Samoa, Tutuila (Powell!). Far different from the species of the preceding section in its pellucid, loosely areolate but firm leaves.

Tribus VII. SKITOPHYLLEÆ.—*Folia verticalia margine inferiore in caulem descendente integro, superiore basi fisso caulem equitante.*

I. FISSIDENS, Hedw Caulis simplex, abbreviatus vel elongatus ramosusque Folia bifariam equitantia, carina late alata foliiformi. Flores terminales, laterales vel basilares. Theca lævis, erecta vel inclinata ;

peristomii dentes bifidi. Calyptra parva, dimidiata, vel basi subintegra —A very extensive genus of mostly small and very elegant Mosses, remarkable for the peculiar structure of their leaves, in which the true leaf—lamina vera—is considered to be that part which embraces the stem, and out of the axil of which the inflorescence arises, but beyond the apex of this, and along its keel the leaf is so expanded that when the stems are viewed laterally, the whole leaf appears as if flat, and inserted vertically upon the stem.

1. *F. lagenarius*, Mitt Journ. of the Proceed Linn. Soc 1868, p. 184; monoicus, pusillus, folia circiter 10-juga, patentia, oblongo-linearia, acuta, nervo pellucido percursa, lamina vera usque ad medium producta, apice subæquali, una cum lamina dorsali apicalique limbo carente minutissime crenata, cellulis minutis rotundis inter se remotiusculis vix obscuris minute papillosis; pedunculus foliis superioribus æquilongus; theca inclinata, cylindracea, pallida, laxe areolata, post operculi conico-subulati delapsum infra os constricta sublageniformi; peristomium dentibus teneris luteis brevibus irregularibus.—Samoa Islands, Tutuila, on *Cyathea leucolepis*, Mett, 1000–2000 ft (Powell! 22) —The entire plant is about three lines high. From *F. scabrisetus* this species differs, in its less obscure leaves, and in the elongated capsule.

2 *F inconspicuus*, Mitt. l c p. 185; monoicus, pusillus; folia circiter 6-juga, patentia, lineari-lanceolata, acuminata, nervo pellucido percurrente, lamina vera usque ad medium producta subæquali, omnibus laminarum marginibus crenulatis, limbo carente, cellulis minutis rotundis pallidis obscuris papillosis; theca in pedunculo breviusculo, parva, obovata, inclinata, operculo subulato.—Samoa, Tutuila and Upolu, on *Cyathea leucolepis*, 1000–2000 ft. (Powell! n. 121) —Stems with the leaves about a line high. Pale green or rusty brown Seta half as long again as the leaves

3. *F. scabrisetus*, Mitt l. c, monoicus; caulis elongatus; folia circiter 12-juga, patentia, approximata, elliptico-lanceolata, nervo angusto pellucido percurrente, lamina vera ad medium usque producta subæquali, a basi usque ad medium hyalino-limbata, lamina dorsali basi rotundata, marginibus ubique tenuissime crenulatis, cellulis minutis obscuris viridibus minutissime papillosis; theca in pedunculo brevi aspero, ovalis, inclinata, operculo subulato obliquo, flos masculus in axillis foliorum superiorum —Samoa Islands, Tutuila (Powell! n 63) —Stems about 4 lines high, and with the leaves about 1 line wide The seta is about a line or a line and a half long The capsule with vesicular cells and a red mouth

4 *F abbreviatus* (sp nov), Mitt; monoicus, caulis brevis, semilinearis; folia 4-8-juga, approximata, patentia, elliptico-lanceolata, acuta, nervo pellucidiore percursa, lamina vera usque ad medium producta apice subæqualis usque ad medium ejus longitudinis tenui hyalino-limbata, lamina dorsali basi decurrente apicalique subintegerrima, cellulis minutis obscuris lævibus; theca in pedunculo brevi pallido, ovalis, erecta, operculo subulato obliquo; peristomium dentibus rubris. Flos masculus vel terminalis vel in ramulo brevissimo basilaris —Raoul Island (M'Gillivray! in Herb. Hooker). A minute species, different from any of the preceding.

TRIBUS I. DICRANEÆ.—Folia viridia, sæpe elongata, angusta, nitida, nervo sæpe dilatato, cellulis basilaribus ad angulos sæpe majoribus coloratis. Peristomii dentes integri vel furcati.

The following five genera of this tribe are represented in Polynesia, but have not yet been found in Viti, viz —I. CERATODON: 1 *C. purpureus*, L Sp Pl p 1574 (*Mnium*), from St Paul's Island (Milne!), Isle of Pines (Strange) II HOLOMITRIUM: 1, *H vaginatum*, Hook. Musc. Exot t. 64 (*Trichostomum*), et Schw. t 309, from Tahiti (Menzies!) III. DICRANUM. 1, *D Sandwichense*, Sull. United St Expl Exped 1859, p 3, var. β condensatum, caulibus abbreviatis (1-2-uncialibus) robustis, foliis confertis; var γ. elongatum, caulibus elongatis (10-12-uncialibus), foliis dissitis patentissimis, from Kaala Mountains (Oahu), β Mauna Kea, Hawaii; γ banks of the Crater, East Maui, Hawaiian Islands; 2, *D. speirophyllum*, Mont. Voy. de la Bonite Crypt p. 275, from Sandwich Islands (Gaudichaud!). IV. CAMPYLOPUS. 1, *C umbellatus*, W. Arnott, Disp 34 (*Trichostomum umbellatum*, Schw. Gaudich. and Freyc. p 224), from Hawaii, on the volcano (Macrae! Haines!), Oahu (Beechey! Seemann! Gaudichaud!); 2, *C introflexus*, Hedw. Sp Musc. t 29 (*Dicranum*), from St. Paul's Island (Milne! Strange!), Isle of Pines (Strange!) V LEUCOLOMA: 1, *L. tenuifolium*, Mitt Linn Soc. Journ. 1868, p. 192, from Tutuila and Upolu, on trees (Powell! n 98)

I. **Dicranella**, C. Muller, Syn. vol. i. p. 430 (*Angstrœmeæ* ejusd. sect.), Schimp. Syn. p. 69. Caulis erectus, apice fertilis. Folia cellulis elongatis areolata. Theca brevis, plus minus ovalis, plicata vel lævis, erecta vel inæqualis, in pedunculo recto vel curvato. Peristomium dentibus 16 brevibus solidis vel irregulari modo fissis. Calyptra dimidiata.—Musci terrestres, humiles, caulibus ut plurimum simplicibus, foliis parvis brevibus angustis mollibus, thecis parvis collibus æqualiter contractis vel callosis inæqualibus.

A genus containing a great number of small Mosses, more abundant in species in South America than elsewhere, those species with erect and smooth capsules approaching very nearly to *Cynontodium*, Hedw., or, as the species belonging to the group so named have been more recently designated, *Leptotrichum*, Hampe, notwithstanding that this last has already been used for a group of *Fungi*, and that Hedwig's genus was founded on species which may be said to be typical species of *Leptotrichum*, but from these species the *Dicranelia* are usually distinguishable by their short, frequently plicate capsule, and shorter not filiform peristomial teeth From the various groups of species comprised in the genus *Dicranum*, this genus differs in the small stature of the species, and in the entire absence of alary cells, the species with curved setæ simulate very nearly the smaller species of the genus *Campylopus*, but differ from this in the same respects as they do from *Dicranum*

1. D. flaccidula, Mitt. in Seem. Bonpl. 1861, p 365 (*Leptotrichum*); dioica, cæspitosa, caulis humilis, simplex; folia patentia stricta vel subsecunda a basi sensim angustata sublanceolata apice subacuta integerrima mollia subnitida, nervo viridi percurrente ubique a folii lamina distincto, cellulis elongatis angustis mollibus, perichætialia paulo majora subconformia, theca in pedunculo gracili erecto aurantiaco elliptico-ovalis, ore parvo operculo subulato recto, annulo lato; peristomium dentibus brevibus solidis —Viti (Seemann!) Also in Tutuila, Samoan Islands, on muddy banks (Powell! n. 15).

A small species with thin soft foliage, more nearly allied to the tropical African *D nitidula*, Mitt. Trans Linn. Soc vol xxiii t 5. f 1, than to any other
Tab 98 *a* Fig 1, plants of the natural size; 2, a leaf from the stem, 3, a perichætial leaf, 4, the capsule and its operculum; 5, a portion of the peristome, all magnified

1. D. trichophylla, Mitt in Seem. Bonpl. 1861, p. 366 (*Leptotrichum*); dioica; caulis simplex vel furcatus, plus minus elongatus; folia basi erecta quadrata vaginantia, cellulis inferioribus elongatis pellucidis areolata, nervo in subulam angustam trichoideam flexuosam integerrimam excurrente, basin versus anguste lamina folii marginata, perichætialia ad basin partis subulatæ paululo latiora; theca in pedunculo humido cygneo-curvato pendula, sicca spiraliter flexo suberecta, ovali-elliptica, inæquali plicata, basi callosa, infra os parvum subobliquum contracta, operculo subulato obliquo, annulo lato, peristomio dentibus angustis dicranis.—Viti (Seemann! 862 part), Ovalau (Milne! in Herb. Hooker, 356 *a*).

Stems ½ to 1½ in high Leaves dull brownish-green, little altered when dry. Allied in the form of its leaves to *D proscripta*, Hsch, but very different in appearance and in its capsule. from *D euphoroclada* and *D nana*, C. Mueller, from Java, it differs in the more exactly quadrate dilated base of its leaves
Tab 98 *b*. Fig 1, plant of the natural size, 2, a leaf showing at the side the areolation and a cross-section; 3, a capsule, with operculum and calyptra, 4, a portion of the peristome, all magnified.

Tribus II. **LEUCOBRYEÆ.**—Folia albida, e nervo maxime dilatato formata. Peristomii dentes integri vel dicrani.

II. **Octoblepharum,** Hedw. Musc Frond. vol. iii. p. 15; caulis erectus, apice fertilis. Folia undique æqualia vel tristicha, nervo sæpe incrassato planiusculo, perichætialia parum diversiformia. Theca plus minus longe pedunculata, erecta, lævis. Peristomium dentibus 16 vel 8. Calyptra cucullata. *Leucophanes*, Brid. vol. i. p. 763.

The following species have not yet been found in Viti —1 *O. dentatum*, Mitt Linn. Soc. Journ 1868, p 178—Samoan Islands, Upolu, near the crater called Tafūa-ā-Upolu, 1000 ft. (Powell! n. 19); taller and with more recurved leaves than *O Schimperi* (*Arthrocormus*), Dozy et Molk Musc Archip Ind. t 27. Tab. 98 *c*, Fig 1, plant of the natural size, 2, a leaf with three cross-sections at different parts of its length, the point and a portion near the base more enlarged. all magnified 2. *O albidum*, Linn Sp. Plant 1583 (*Bryum*)—Sandwich Islands (Lay et Collie!) 3. *O incrassatum* (sp nov), Mitt mss; cæspitosum, caulis humilis, folia densa, a basi angusto oblonga, erecta, e cellulis oblongis areolata et limbo angusto marginata, in subulam crassam trigonam lævem apice obtusiusculo oblique acuto serrulato producta, nervo in parte oblonga ⅓ folii latitudinis in subula trigona totam occupante; medio e stratis cellularum superimpositarum 5 formato —Samoan Islands, Tutuila (Powell!); closely resembling *O dentatum*, but with leaves more straight and not so much narrowed at the points, the margins of the trigonous upper portion more pellucid, so as to give the idea of their having a narrow lamina, of which, however, on making a cross-section, there is no trace, and the limbation of the base is narrower, a few oblong septate brown bodies have been seen attached to the apices of the leaves, similar to those observable in *Syrrhopodon* and *Calymperes.* Tab 98 *g.* Fig 1, plant of the natural size; 2, a leaf, with a portion near the base, more enlarged, a cross-section of the upper part and the point as seen laterally, all magnified 4 *O. asperum*, Mitt Linn. Soc Journ. 1868, p 178 — Samoan Islands, Upolu, on trees, 1000 ft. (Powell ! n 113). Tab. 98 *d.* Fig 1, plant of the natural size; 2, a leaf, with portions more enlarged, and two cross-sections, all magnified 5. *O. scabrum*, Mitt. Linn Soc. Journ 1868, p 178.—Samoan Islands, Tutuila (Powell ! n. 126). Tab. 98 *f.* Fig. 1, stem of the natural size, 2, a leaf with two cross-sections, and portions showing the structure at the respective parts, all magnified. 6. *O. recurvum*, Mitt. Linn. Soc. Journ. 1868, p. 179.—Samoan Islands, Tutuila (Powell ! n 104).

1. **O. scolopendrium**, Mitt. in Bonpl. 1861, p. 366 (*Syrrhopodon*); cæspitosum; caulis elongatus, subsimplex, erectus; folia usque ad medium eorum longitudinis cauli appressa, sese amplectantia, inde subulata, squarroso-patentia vel recurva, siccitate immutata, nervo rigido subtereti denticulis papillisque scaberrimo carinata, margine limbo incrassato dense papilloso denticulato apicem versus denticulis validioribus armato ibique cum nervo confluente, cellulis omnibus hyalinis quadratis trapezoideisque areolata.—Viti (Seemann ! n. 813).

Three inches high or more, very nearly resembling *Syrrhopodon tristichus,* but more rigid, and with leaves of a very different structure.

Tab. 98 *e.* Fig. 1, stem of the natural size; 2, a leaf, with the point further enlarged, and cross-sections and portions showing the structure opposite the respective parts, all magnified.

2. **O. smaragdinum**, Mitt. Bonpl. 1861, p. 366; cæspitosum; caulis humilis; folia a basi erectiore laxe appressa, patentia, elongate lanceolata, lineali-attenuata, apice latiuscula, acuta, subcarinata, nervo basi folii latitudinis tertiam partem occupante, in partem superiorem patentem totam folii constituente, linea angusta obscuriore percursa, e stratis duobus cellularum superimpositarum composito, margine basi angustissime limbata, apice et per carinam apicem versus serrulata, cellulis laminæ folii rhombeis.—Viti (Seemann ! inter n. 863).

Similar to *O. densifolium,* but with the areolation of the nerve more obscure and greener, and the cells smaller

Tab 98 *i* Fig 2, plant of the natural size; 1, a leaf with various portions, including two cross-sections, all magnified.

3. **O. densifolium**, Mitt. Bonpl. 1861, p. 366 (*Leucophanes*); cæspitosum; caulis elongatus, ramosus; folia dense inserta, elongate lanceolata, inferne erecta, superne patentia squarrosave, subcomplicata, apice obtusa, serrulata, mucrone parvo angusto, nervo totum folii constituente e cellularum stratis duobus composito ad margines inferiores, limbo angusto e cellularum elongatarum seriebus circiter tribus formato circumdata; theca in pedunculo longiusculo, oblongo-cylindracea.—Viti (Seemann ! inter 862; Milne ! in Herb. Hooker).

Tab 98 *h.* Fig. 1, plant of the natural size; 2, a leaf, with a portion showing the cells at the margin, also a cross-section, magnified.

III. **Leucobryum**, Hampe, Linnæa, xiii. p. 42. Caulis erectus, apice fertilis vel inferne procumbens, e ramulo brevissimo laterali fructiferus. Folia undique æqualia vel pentasticha, marginibus superne involutis. Theca in pedunculo elongato, inæqualis, horizontalis, plicata, operculo longirostro. Peristomium dentibus dicranis. Calyptra cucullata.

The following are Polynesian species, as yet not found in Viti, viz —1. *L glaucum*, Linn Sp Plant. 1582 (*Bryum*)—Sandwich Islands (Gaudichaud !). 2. *L* (*Pegophyllum*) *Seemanni* (sp nov), Mitten, caulis elongatus, furcatim ramosus; folia falcata, ad latera cauli arcte appressa, secunda, linealilanceolata, sensim angustata, lævia, apice obtusiusculo acuto parce dentato, marginibus supra folii medium involutis, lamina folii e cellulis angustis inferne in seriebus 6–8 dispositis infra apicem evanida, cellulis nervi oblongis rectangulis, cellulis alaribus obsoletis —Oahu (Seemann! Herb Hooker) —Stems 2-3 inches high. Leaves 3 lines or more long, so strongly laterally compressed that the stems are flattened, not altered in the dry state, of a very pale fulvous-green nearly white, and with an almost satin-like gloss. This fine Moss comes nearer to *L Javense* than to any of the numerous species of the Indian Archipelago, but from this it differs greatly in appearance on account of its compressed foliage. 4. *L. rugosum*, Mitt Linn Soc Journ vol x —Samoa Islands. Manua, on trees (Powell! n 101) 5. *L. Javense*, Beauv. Prodr. p 88 (*Sphagnum*) —Sandwich Islands (Lay et Collie!)

1. **L. sanctum**, Hampe; Dozy et Molk. Bryol. Javan t. 12; caules in cæspitem laxum mollem congesti; folia subsecunda, recta vel falcata, a basi erectiore oblonga, concava, patentia, subulata, lævia, apice obtusiuscule acuta, paucidentata, margine involuta, lamina folii angustissima, e cellulis elongatis angustis in seriebus 3–5 dispositis infra apicem desinente, cellulis nervi oblongis rectangulis; folia perichætialia a basi ovali anguste subulata, acuta; theca in pedunculo elongato brevis, subhorizontalis, plicata, basi strumosa, operculo subulato; peristomii dentes furcati —Viti (Milne!). Also in Samoa, Upolu, on trees, 1200 ft. (Powell! n. 82), Pacific Islands (Beechey!); Aneitum (Milne! 368, Herb. Hooker).

A very soft species, with its leaves most usually somewhat falcate, but this is less evident in the Samoan specimens

2. **L. laminatum**, Mitt in Bonplandia, 1861, p 366; cæspites densi; folia dorso rugosa, margine lamina distincta marginata, apicem versus minute serrata —Viti (Seemann! n. 844).

In size, this Moss resembles the *L. aduncum*, Dozy et Molk Bryol. Javan. t. 11, but its leaves are wider above the middle than in that species, and the lamina is more distinct

TRIBUS III. **SYRRHOPODONTEÆ.**—Folia viridia, obscura, cellulis inferioribus in medio folio hyalinis. Peristomii dentes parvi, integri vel divisi.

A tribe of tropical Mosses, easily distinguishable by the hyaline enlarged cells occupying a greater or less space in the base of the leaves

IV. **Syrrhopodon**, Schw. Suppl. ii. 100. Calyptra lævis, dimidiata.

The following have not yet been gathered in Viti, viz. —1. *S Platyceru* (sp nov), Mitt , pusillus , caulis humilis; folia a basi erectiora, patentia, anguste lanceolato-linealia, subligulata, apice obtuse acuta, margine superne flexuosa, apice minute denticulata, nervo pellucido percursa, cellulis hyalinis usque ad ⅔ folii longitudinis productis inde ad apicem minutis rotundis glauco-viridibus, theca in pedunculo gracillimo ovalis, operculo subulato eam superante, peristomii dentibus validis —Lord Howe's Island, on *Platycerium* (M'Gillivray and Milne! Herb. Hooker).—A small species like *S. Gaudichaudi*, Schw., from South America, but with leaves more narrow, the limb distinct all round the margin, and, when dry, not closely contorted and appressed, but loosely erecto-patent —Tab 98 *j* Fig 1, plant of the natural size, 2, a leaf and the apex further enlarged; 3, the capsule, with operculum and calyptra; 4, portion of peristome —all magnified. 2 *S involutus*, Schw. t 132 —Pacific Islands (Herb. Hooker!); Samoa (Powell!); also in the Island of Banca (ex Herb Van der Sande Lacoste!) 3. *S rufescens*, Hook. et Grev in Brewster's Edinb Journ. of Sc iii. p 227 —Marian Islands (Gaudichaud!); found also at Singapore and in the Island of Labuan 4 *S gracilis* (sp nov), Mitt., humilis, laxe cæspitosus, ramosus, folia a basi obovata erecta, cellulis hyalinis areolata, margine superne limbo bi-tridentato interdum integerrimo circumdata, exinde patentia, lineali-ligulata, obtusa, breviter acuminata, nervo lævi pellucidiore percursa, limbo angusto hyalino integerrimo marginata, cellulis minutis rotundis obscuris papillis intus extusque prominulis scaberrimis; pedunculus gracillimus, elongatus, theca minuta, ovalis.—Pacific Islands (Milne), growing with a specimen of *S. croceus* —A very small species, of a pale whitish colour. Tab 98 *k*. Fig 1, plant of the natural size; 2, a leaf, with a portion further enlarged to show the hyaline margin and a cross-section —magnified. 5 *S croceus*, Mitt Linn Soc. Journ 1859 —Samoan Islands, Tutuila, and all the islands, on trees, (2000-2500 feet), Powell, n. 12 Tab 98 *n* Fig 1, stem of the natural size, 2, a leaf, with cross-section and portions further enlarged opposite the respective parts.—all magnified 6 *S glauco-virens*, Mitt. Linn Soc Journ. 1868, p 176 —Samoan Islands, Tutuila, and Upolu, on trees (Powell! n. 99). Tab 98 *m*. Fig. 1, stem of the natural size, 2, a leaf, with a cross-section and portions more enlarged opposite the respective parts —all magnified. 7. *S strictifolius* (sp nov), Mitt; caulis humilis, folia a basi erecta, obovata, margine integerrima, cellulis hyalinis areolata, patentia, anguste lineali-elongata, stricta, haud canaliculata, apice obtuso acuta, limbo crasso tereti scabro marginata, nervo crasso sub summo apice desinente, cellulis minutis rotundis obscuris areolata.—Samoan Islands, Tutuila (Powell!)—Like *S. glauco-virens*, but with narrower, more rigid leaves. Tab. 98 *l.* Fig 1, stem of the natural size; 2, a leaf, with a cross-section and a portion more enlarged to show the structure:—all magnified. 8. *S. Mülleri*, Dozy et Molk. Bryol. Javan. t. 42 (*Calymperidium*).—Samoa, Upolu, on trees (Powell! n. 120). 9 *S aristifolius*, Mitt. Journ. of the Proceed Linn. Soc. 1868, p. 176.—Samoan Islands, Upolu, on trees, 1000-2000 ft. (Powell! 89) 10. *S. fasciculatus*, Hook et Grev. Schw t. 299 —Samoan Islands (Powell!), Pitcairn's Island (Herb. Hooker), also in Borneo (Motley!), Ternate (Dickson!), Chili (Cuming!), Malay Peninsula (Wallich!) 11 *S constrictus*, Sull. Amer. Expl. Exp 1859, p. 6 —Sandwich Islands, South Sea Islands (Nightingale! Herb Hooker), Samoan Islands, Tutuila (Powell! n 49). 12. *S. crassinervis*, Mitt. Journ of the Proceed Linn. Soc. 1868, p 189.—Samoa, Tutuila, on bark of trees (Powell! n. 129).

* *Eusyrrhopodon.*—Caulis erectus. Folia limbo pallido vel hyalino marginata.

† Folia basi integerrima.

1. **S. albovaginatus,** Schw. t. 131; dioicus; caulis humilis, laxe cæspitosus; folia inter se remotiuscula, dimidio inferiore erecta, e cellulis hyalinis areolata, dimidio superiore patentia divergentiaque lineali-ligulata, strictiuscula, planiuscula, sicca recurva, apice obtusa, margine limbo angusto apice denticulato circumdata et in parte superiore anguste inflexa, nervo percurrente dorso papillis aspero, cellulis obscuris papillis grossiusculis aculeiformibus prominulis; theca in pedunculo gracili ovali cylindracea, operculo subulato breviore.—Viti (Milne! Herb. Hooker), Samoa (Powell!), Rauwack (Gaudichaud!), Isle of Pines (Strange!).

2. **S. lævigatus** (sp. nov.), Mitt.; caulis gracilis, elongatus, parum divisus, laxe cæspitosus; folia tristicha, tertio parte inferiore eorum longitudinis erecta, latiora, complicata, e cellulis hyalinis teneris areolata, limbo cartilagineo lævi marginata, exinde patentia lineali-subulata canaliculata, nervo crassiusculo intus lævi extus versus apicem dentibus hyalinis remotiusculis armato, cæteroquin lævi, margine limbo cartilagineo apicem versus denticulato circumdata, cellulis minutis rotundis glauco-viridibus obscuris; theca in pedunculo breviusculo (3-lineari) oblongo elliptica, fusca.—*S. tristichus*, Mitt. in Linn. Soc. Journ. 1868, p. 176.—Ovalau (Milne! in Herb Hooker), Samoa, on trees near the crater of Tafua-a Upolu, 1000 ft. (Powell! n. 74).

In external appearance closely resembling *S. tristichus*, Nees, Bryol Javan. t 44, but in that species the nerve throughout the patent portion of the leaf, and for a short distance below it, is equally erose with densely placed minute dentiform papillæ.

3 **S. luteus,** Mitt. Journ. of the Proceed. Linn. Soc. 1868, p 188; rami elongati, laxe cæspitosi; folia a basi brevi erectiore ad insertionem constricta, superne parum latiora, patentia, sicca contorta subsecunda, linearia, elongata, sensim acuminata, nervo percurrente, margine undulata serrulata, limbo inferne latiore apicem versus evanido, cellulis hyalinis spatium parvum occupantibus, reliquis omnibus parvis anguloso-rotundatis obscuriusculis, papillis inconspicuis parietibus pellucidioribus; folia perichætialia erectiora, caulinis similia; theca in pedunculo brevi cylindracea.—Ovalau, on stones in the mountains (Milne!); also Samoa, Tutuila (Powell! 106)

A little more slender than *S fasciculatus*, with narrower leaves, more acute at their points, and scarcely dilated at their bases.

V. **Calymperes,** Sw. Spreng. et Link, Jahrb. 1818, vol. i. t. 1. Calyptra plicata, basi amplexans, apicem versus fissura laterali operiens. Folia lata, subspathulata, sicca contracta.—*Hyophilina*, C. Mueller, Syn. vol. i. p. 523.

A genus corresponding in all respects with *Syrrhopodon*, excepting only the calyptra, which is larger, strongly plicate, and opens by a longitudinal fissure for the egress of the spores. The following species have not yet been found in Viti, viz.:—1 *C Dozyanum*, Mitt Linn. Soc Journ 1859 (*C Moluccense*, Dozy et Molk. Bryol Javan t. 37).—Samoan Islands, Tutuila (Powell! n. 18); found also in Java, and a specimen was marked by Dickson as received from India Stems seldom more than half an inch high, more frequently shorter; leaves when dry incurved, the margins involute, with no trace of the callous limb 2 *O porrectum*, Mitt. Linn Soc. Journ. 1868, p 172 —Samoan Islands, Tutuila, on bark (Powell! n 10) Tab 98 *o* Fig 1, stems of the natural size, 2, a leaf, with section and portion enlarged, 3, an anomalous leaf, with section, magnified 3 *C. serratum*, A Braun, Bryol. Javan. t 50.—Samoan Islands, Tutuila, on Tree-ferns (Powell! n 47); also in Java.

1. C. lorifolium, Mitt. Linn. Soc. Journ. 1868, p. 173; dioicum, caulis humilis; folia a basi oblonga, latiora, cellulis hyalinis quadratis distinctis fere ad apicem usque areolata, ad latera fascia latiuscula e cellulis parvis angustis elongatis firmis, et limbo tenerrimo e cellulis apicibus exstantibus crenulato marginata, subito contracta, longe loriformia, erecto-patentia, sicca laxe curvata subcrispata, apice acuminata, nervo percurrente, limbo obscuro parum incrassato remote serrulato apice paucidenticulato circumducta, cellulis incrassatis pellucidis rotundatis oblatisque; folia perichætialia conformia, apicibus ad orificium thecæ cylindraceæ attingentibus; pedunculus ruber, operculum conico-subulatum; calyptra plicata, apice acuminata, scabra, basi infra thecam descendens, torta.— Viti (Milne!). Also Samoan Islands, Manua, on *Alsophila lunulata*, on the ascent of the Olotane mountain, 1400 feet (Powell! 47), and in Borneo.

2. C. Taitense, Sull Amer. Expl. Exped. 1859, p. 6. t. 4 (*Syrrhopodon*); caulis laxe cæspitosus, elongatus; folia densa, a basi erecta parum latiore patentia, ligulata, planiuscula, apice subito contracta, obtusa, nervo crassiusculo in mucronem crassum lamina folii angusta marginatum apice cupuliferum producto, limbo basi angusto lamina tenui angustissimo crenulato marginato supra basin erectiore obscuro extus biangulato angulis breviter serrulatis usque ad acuminis basin producto, cellulis hyalinis ad apicem usque partis erectioris continuatis, cellulis superioribus minutis rotundis obscuris; folia perichætialia conformia, apicibus vix ad thecæ cylindricæ os attingentibus, operculum subulatum; calyptra angulis scabris —Viti, damp places in high ground (Milne! 352, Herb. Hooker), Aneitum (Milne!), Samoan Islands, Tutuila (Powell! n. 25), Tahiti (American Exploring Expedition).

TRIBUS IV. **HYPOPTERYGIEÆ.**—Caulis primarius repens, ramos ascendentes vel erectos inferne stipitiformes superne in frondem erectam vel horizontalem divisi. Folia dimorpha, majora disticha oblique inserta asymmetrica, minora symmetrica transversim inserta. Theca in pedunculo exserta, peristomio perfecto vel ciliis carentibus. Calyptra dimidiata Genus unicum.

VI. **Hypopterygium,** Brid.

The following two species are not yet represented in Viti —1 *H. oceanicum*, Mitt. in Hook. Handb Fl N. Zealand, pt. 2. p. 487 —Kermadec Islands, Raoul Island, and Sunday Island (Milne and M'Gillivray!), Norfolk Island (Cunningham and Dr. Thomson! Herb Hooker) 2 *H.* (*Euhypopterygium*) *flaccidum* (sp nov), Mitt.; stipes elongatus, viridis, sparsifolius, supra in frondem flabelliformem ramosum divisus, folia ramea divaricata, ovali-ovata, obtuse acuta, nervo supra medium evanido margine limbo e cellularum seriebus tribus conflatis formato superne denticulis brevibus serrato circumdata, cellulis ellip- tico-ovalibus areolata; folia stipuliformia orbiculata, nervo in mucronem excurrente —Pacific Islands (collector unknown)—Stems 1½ inch high Frond 1 inch wide Leaves yellowish-green Very similar to *H Vriesii*, Bryol Javan t 110, but with leaves not so acute, more flaccid, and more pellucid.

1. H. (*Lopidium*) **struthiopteris,** Brid. vol. ii. p. 716; rami erecti vel adscendentes, inferne substipitati, superne pennæformi-pinnati; folia majora sublanceolato-ligulata, apice latiuscula, nervo concolori in mucronem brevem excurrente, margine integerrima vel subcrenulata basi latere inferiore inflexa, cellulis parvis rotundis areolata; folia minora parva, lanceolata.—Viti (Seemann!).

The specimen consists only of a single stem, but it corresponds with those received from Java

Tribus V. **RHACOPILEÆ.**—Folia inæqualia, biformia, omnia siccatione sursum involuta, pagina interiore ad caules latus superius spectante.

The following genus has not yet been found in Viti:—1. Powellia, Mitt. Linn. Soc. Journ vol x p 187, *P involutifolia*, Mitt l c —Samoan Islands, Tutuila, on a Cocoanut-tree a little inland; Fangasá Bay (1–2 feet) (Powell l n 43).

VII. **Rhacopilum,** Beauv. Prodr. p 36. Caules prostrati, radicantes, parum vel subpinnatim ramosi. Folia diversiformia, in caulis latere superiore minora, stipuliformia Fructus e caulis latere oriundus; theca in pedunculo trigono elongato cylindracea, suberecta horizontalisve, demum plicata, peristomio perfecto, calyptra dimidiata vel plurifida sæpe pilosa.—Musci terrestres v. in arborum truncis putridis degentes, cæspites latos depressos formantes, foliis intense viridibus siccitate incurvis.

A genus well distinguished by the peculiarity of its leaves being of a different form on the upper side of the stems from those which are inserted on the lower side, these latter, too, have always their inner surface turned upwards, so that, at first sight, their insertion might be supposed to be distichous All the species are very similar, but differ in size and some minute particulars.

1. **R. spectabile,** Reinw. et Hsch. Bryol. Javan. t. 144 et 115; dioicum; folia majora late ovata acuta margine serrata nervo in mucronem excurrente, minora basi ovata lanceolata, omnia cellulis rotundis vel ovali-rotundatis areolata, perichætialia ovato-lanceolata subulato-attenuata integerrima; theca longe pedunculata, elongata, horizontalis, demum deflexa, basi substrumosa.—Viti (Seemann!) Also Samoa and Tutuila (Powell l n. 65).

These specimens differ a little from the common state of the species found in Java in having the areolation rather more lax, but in size and appearance they correspond closely.

2. **R. cuspidigerum,** Schw. in Freycinet, Voyage, 1826, p. 227; dioicum?; folia majora ovata obtusiuscula margine subintegerrima plus minus incurva convolutacea, minora ovato-lanceolata, omnia nervo in mucronem excurrente cellulis parvis densis rotundis obscure areolata.—*R. convolutum*, C. Mueller, Syn. ii. p. 13?—Viti (Milne!). Also in Sandwich Islands (Gaudichaud), Samoa and Tutuila (Powell l n. 39), Norfolk Island (Thompson!), Isle of Pines (Strange! M'Gillivray!)

The original specimens gathered by Gaudichaud are rather smaller and more compact than those from the other localities, but there does not appear to be any definite character whereby they may be distinguished from the states so frequently included in collections from Australia, Tasmania, and New Zealand. The leaves are entire or irregularly crenulate.

Tribus VI. **HOOKERIEÆ.**—Folia inæqualia, seriebus utrinque 2 lateralibus longioribus sæpe verticaliter planis, seriebus reliquis minoribus appressis, rarius æqualia. Calyptra mitriformis.

The following genus has not yet been found in Viti, viz :—Pilotrichum: 1, *P. rugifolium*, C Mueller, Syn ii p. 177 —Hawaii (Menzies, in Herb Hooker, where also is another specimen from Dickson without locality).

VIII. **Hookeria,** Sm. Caulis procumbens, vage vel pinnatim ramosus. Folia binervia vel enervia, diversiformia.

1. **H. papillata,** Mont. Ann. des Sc. Nat. 1845, p. 93 (*Hookeria*); synoica; caules procumbentes, subpinnatim ramosi; folia compressa, superiora media oblonga, intermedia ovata, lateralia ovato-ligulata, omnia apice obtusa breviter apiculata angulatave, margine apicem versus crenulata, nervis fere ad apicem continuis dorso superne serrulatis, cellulis parvis rotundis, papilla inconspicua medio imposita; folia in seriebus inferioribus acutiora, pellucidiora, cellulis suboblongis; perichætialia erecta, inferne ovata, inde ligulata acuta, interna ovata latiora; theca in pedunculo elongato lævi ovalis, horizontalis, collo sensim angustato; calyptra scabra.—*H. oblongifolia*, Sull. Proceed. of the

3 E 2

Amer. Acad. of Arts and Sc. 1851; Island of Gau, Viti (Milne!). Also in Samoa (Græffe!) and Tutuila (Powell! n. 69).

Foliage obscure, glaucous green In size, habit, and appearance, this species, which appears to extend through the Indian Archipelago to the Islands of Polynesia, but has not yet been observed in Australia or Tasmania, corresponds closely with the numerous species found on the eastern side of the Andes in S America, in all which there is great uniformity on the foliage, which is generally very obtuse, of a dull obscure æruginous-green, and they form a natural group, which has been elsewhere called *Callicostella*

IX. **Chætomitrium,** Dozy et Molk.   Caulis repens vel procumbens, pinnatim ramosus.   Folia binervia, uniformia

A genus of very elegant species, chiefly found in the Indian Archipelago, one other only is yet known to inhabit Ceylon, they approach very nearly to some forms of *Lepidopilum,* so abundant in tropical America, but differ in habit: in *Chætomitrium* the stems are procumbent and rooting, and the fruit arises from them or from the lower part of the principal branches, in *Lepidopilum* the fruit arises from the upper part of free branches, and the teeth of the outer peristome have usually the external lamina very narrow in proportion to the internal The following species have not yet been found in Viti:—1. *C speciosum,* Sull. Amer Expl Exped. 1859, p 23 t. 22 (*Holoblepharum*)—Samoan Islands (Amer Exped) 2 *C Taitense,* Sull Amer. Expl Exped 1859, p 22 t 23—Society Islands, Mountains of Tahiti (Amer Expl Exped) 3 *C. depressum,* Mitt Journ. of the Proceed Linn. Soc. 1868, p 190—Samoa, Tutuila, trees in low shady woods, very rare, only once found (Powell! n. 81). 4 *C. frondosum,* Mitt. Journ. of the Proceed Linn Soc. 1868, p 189 —Samoan Islands, Tutuila, on trees by the ascent to Matafao, 1500-2000 ft. (Powell! n. 68).

1 **C. rugifolium,** Sull. Amer. Expl. Exped 1859, p. 23 t. 22 (*Holoblepharum*); dioicum, caulis prostratus, ramis brevibus approximatis, pinnatus; folia compressa, ovato-lanceolata, apicem versus excavata ibique pagina inferiore denticulata, marginibus inflexis constricta, breviter binervia, margine crebre serrulata, cellulis angustis noduliferis; folia perichætialia imbricata, apicibus in cuspidem creberrime denticulatum productis; pedunculus longiusculus, ubique setulis hispidulus; theca ovalis, inclinata, operculo rostrato; calyptra setulis villosa.—Viti, on trees (Amer. Exped.); Ovalau, in the mountains (Milne! n. 364). Also in the Solomon Islands.

X. **Distichophyllum,** Dozy et Molk. Musci Archip. Ind. p. 99.—Caulis erectus ascendens vel procumbens. Folia tenera, uninervia.

The following are Polynesian species of this genus —1. *D Freycineti,* Schw t 279 (*Hypnum*).—Sandwich Islands (Douglas!), Oahu (Beechey!) 2. *D paradoxum,* Mont. Voy de la Bonite, p 296 (*Hookeria Pterygophyllum*) —Oahu (Beechey!); Sandwich Islands (Gaudichaud!) 3. *D.* (*Discophyllum,* Mitt Linn Soc. Journ vol x.) *flavescens,* Mitt. Linn. Soc Journ vol. x p. 191—Samoa, Upolu, on trees (Powell, 93).

1. **D. Vitianum,** Sull. Am. Expl. Exped. t. 24; caulis humilis, simplex vel inferne divisus; folia compressa, media intermediaque parum minora oblongo-ligulata acuta, lateralia spathulata apiculata, nervo infra medium evanido, limbo angusto integerrimo flexuoso e seriebus cellularum duabus composito marginata, cellulis superioribus rotundo-hexagonis, inferioribus ovali-hexagonis; theca in pedunculo brevi papilloso horizontalis; calyptra basi lacero-fimbriata, setulis inspersa.—Ovalau, trees in the mountains (Milne!); Samoan Islands (Powell! n. 94).

Foliage pale glaucous-green, with iridescent cells. This species is allied to the Javan *D spathulatum,* Dozy et Molk

Tribus VII. **NECKEREÆ.**—Fructus in ramis frondiformibus e caule oriundis immersus vel exsertus.

The two following genera have not yet been met with in Viti —I. CALYPTOTHECIUM, Mitt. Linn Soc Journ vol x. 1. *C. prælongum,* Mitt. Linn Soc. Journ vol x p 190.—Society Islands, with fruit (Bidwill, Herb. Hooker), Samoa, Upolu, on trees, barren (Powell! n. 102) Tab 97 Fig. 1, a stem of the natural size, 2, a leaf, 3, perichætium; 4, a portion of the peristome, all magnified. II. ŒDICLADIUM,

Mitt Linn. Soc. Journ. vol. x p. 194. 1. *Œ. involutaceum*, Mitt. Linn. Soc. Journ. vol. x. p. 195.— Samoan Islands, Tutuila (Powell ! n. 140). 2 *Œ. purpuratum* (sp nov.), Mitt , caulis primarius repens, foliis parvis appressis oblongis subulato-acuminatis, ramos crassos in cæspitem demum congestos prodens , folia ramea tumide imbricata, patentia, oblongo-ovalia, margine involutacea, conniventia, inde in subulam loriformem planam apice serrulatam producta, basi brevissime binervia, cellulis angustis ad angulos majoribus fuscis in maculam congestis.—Aneitum, on bark of trees (Milne ! n 373) This fine Moss forms large patches composed of densely tufted branches, about half an inch long, these arise from the closely creeping slender rhizomiform stem, and are of the same thickness as in *Œ rufescens*, Hornsch , although shorter. The foliage is shining green or reddish purple

XI. Crypæa, Brid. Caules primarii repentes radicantes. Rami fertiles eflagelliferi, fructiferi · abbreviati vel elongati. Theca immersa. Calyptra parva, plurifida.

1. **C. gracilis** (sp nov.), Mitt., monoica ; rami elongati, graciles, rigiduli, ramulis inordinatim dispositis pinnatim ramosi ; folia erecto-patentia, laxe imbricata, late ovata, obtusiuscule acuta, margine inferne recurva, superne erecta, apicem versus crenulata, nervo sub apice desinente, cellulis superioribus parvis oblongo-ovalibus, basalibus ad angulos decurrentes rotundatis subquadratisve ad nervum paucis elongatis; fructu ex apicibus ramulorum vel in ramulo brevi e latere ramulorum oriens, theca subsessilis, oblonga, in foliis perichætialibus oblongis subulato-acuminatis acuminibus margine dorsoque serrulatis immersa, operculo depresse conico acuminato; peristomium depressum, dentibus pallidis, internum æquilongum, processibus angustis obscuriusculis; calyptra parva, fusca, apice papulosa.—Viti (Seemann ! Milne !) ; Samoa (E. Græffe ! ex Herb. F. Mueller).

Nearly allied to *C Gorvæana*, Mont , from Chili, but with shorter leaves, and a smaller and more depressed peristome, also to *C. dilatata*, Hook. f et Wils Fl. Nov Zealand, t. 88 f 2, but more slender, with more nearly ovate leaves, and those of the perichætium more than twice as wide.

Tab. 98 P. Fig 1, a stem of the natural size ; 2, leaves with cells more enlarged , 3, the perichætium and capsule , 4, portion of peristome ; 5, calyptra, all magnified.

XII. Spiridens, Nees ab Esenb. Nov. Act. vol. xi. p. 143. Caulis erectus, basi radicans, superne simplex vel plus minus pinnatim divisus. Folia undique inserta, e basi erecta teneriora, laxius areolata, immarginata, amplexante angustata, planiuscula, firma, patentia vel squarrosa, pagina fuscis e duplicibus stratis cellularum compositus striata, limbo incrassato, denticulis parvis serrato-marginata, nervo superne sæpe cum limbo coalito longe producto, inferne sæpe in parte folii erectiore obsoleto, cellulis polymorphis parvis elongatis pentagonis rotundisque immixtis lævibus. Fructus in ramulo brevissimo e superioribus partibus caulium vel ramorum oriens; folia perichætialia parva. Theca magna, breviter pedunculata, operculo rostrato, peristomium magnum externum dentibus firmis elongatis, internum processibus ciliisque angustis in membrana exserta imposita. Calyptra cucullata

The genus *Spiridens* includes a small number of species, but themselves among the largest of Mosses, they appear to grow in a tufted manner, without any trace of creeping stem, and in this particu'ar differ from the equatorial American species of *Prionodon*, with which in many other particulars they agree. All the species correspond very nearly in size, habit, and appearance ; some appear to be almost undivided, others are in the upper part of the stems branched in an irregularly pinnate manner. The leaves are described by Schimper as composed in their upper part of a double layer of cells, but this only occurs where the leaves are marked with thickened bands, and these are sometimes absent, so that the normal structure is, as usual among Mosses, a single stratum The following two species have not yet been found in Viti, viz.—1. *S capilliferus*, Mitt. Linn Soc. Journ. vol. x. p. 194, from Samoa, Tutuila, on Tree-ferns, 1500–2000 ft. (Powell ! n. 128) Tab. 97. Fig. 1, a stem of the natural size ; 2, a leaf, magnified. 2. *S Vieillardi*, Schimp , Spiridens Revis p 9 t 2, from New Caledonia (Dr. Vieillard), Pacific Islands (Nightingale ! Herb. Hooker) ; this is the only species yet known in which cilia are present between the processes of the internal peristome

1. **S. aristifolius,** Mitt. Linn. Soc. Journ. vol. x. p 193 , caulis elongatus, superne plus minus

ramosus; folia a basi ovali erecta, recurva, patentia, subulata, sensim in acumen aristiforme sub-teres attenuata, dentibus aculeiformibus ad apicem aristæ minoribus brevioribusque serratis incrassatis; lamina folii supra basin erectam transversim rugulosa; perichætialia a basi ovali inferne enervi convoluta, superne in aristam thecam oblongam curvatam superantem producta, apice remote dentata, operculum subulatum, peristomium dentibus pallidis angustis elongatis, internum processibus parum brevioribus in membrana ad ½ dentium longitudinis exserta impositis.—Viti (Milne!); Samoan Islands, Tutuila, and Upolu (Powell! n. 127).

This species corresponds generally with *S Reinwardti*, Nees, from the Moluccas, but its leaves are more attenuated into a bristly point.

Tab. 97　Fig 1, a stem of the natural size; 2, leaves with portions more enlarged, 3, perichætium and capsule, 4, a portion of the peristome, all magnified

2. S. flagellosus, Schimp. Nova Acta, vol. xxxiii. t. 4, caulis superne ramosus; rami patentes apice attenuati, ramulos flagelliformes attenuatos prodentes; folia caulina a basi latiora, erecta, patentia divergentiaque, subulata, apicibus rectis vel incurvis, siccitate semitorta curvataque; nervo cum marginibus incrassatis denticulis pluribus parvis angustis serratis coalito, in acumen elongatum trigonum sublæve continuo, pagina inferne fasciis obscurioribus striata; folia in ramulis flagelli-formibus erecto-patentibus pallidioribus striata; fructus *S. aristifolio* simile, peristomio interno membrana basilari latiore.—Viti (Seemann! n. 840, Wilkes); Aneitum (Milne!); Isle of Pines (Strange!)

The erect portion of the leaf in this species is much dilated, being half as wide again when spread out as the patent part　The fruit is described from Dr. Schimper's figure.

Tab 97. Fig. 1, stem of the natural size; 2, a leaf, with portion more enlarged, magnified.

3. S. Balfourianus, Grev. Ann. and Mag. of Nat. Hist. 1848, t 18; caulis superne ramis patentibus irregularibus subfasciculatim pinnatus, folia a basi versus insertionem angustata, erectiora, sensim patentia, siccitate curvata subcontorta, ambitu late ovali-lanceolata, subulato-acuminata, fasciis paucis angustis striata, nervo apice cum limbo coalito in acumen aristiforme producto dentibus marginalibus minutis brevibus usque ad apicem continuatis.—Viti (Milne!), Tahiti (Sibbald! Collie!); Society Islands (Bidwill in Herb. Hooker).

Some of the specimens very much branched above, in size and appearance nearly resembling *S flagellaris*, but with leaves having their erect portion not dilated, and at the base very much narrowed, and the patent upper part twice as wide as in that species　Schimper in his monograph of *Spiridens*, figures the leaf of *S. Balfourianus* with large and leafy teeth, a character in opposition to that given by Greville, who figures it narrower than in *S Reinwardti*

XIII. Pterobryum, Hornsch.　Rami fertiles inferne simplices, stipitiformes, superne in frondem pinnatam arbusculosamve ramosam divisi.　Folia undique æqualia vel compressa.　Theca immersa vel exserta, peristomio parvo depresso, dentibus inter se et cum peristomii interni rudimentis cohæ-rentibus　Calyptra parva, integra

The following Polynesian species have as yet not been met with in Viti, viz —1. *P. cylindraceum*, Mont Ann des Sc. Nat 1848, p. 109, from Pacific Islands (Beechey!), Samoa, Tutuila (Powell! n. 72)　2. *P Mauiense*, Sull Amer Expl. Exp p 21 t. 19 (*Meteorium*), from Sandwich Islands, East Maui, on the north bank of the crater, 10,200 ft. (Amer Exp); Samoa, Tutuila (Powell!)

1. P. Vitianum, Sull. in Proceed. of the Amer. Acad. of Arts and Sciences, 1855 (*Pilotrichum*), dioicum; rami inferne simplices, superne in frondem arbusculosam pinnatim divisi; folia nitida, quinquefaria, imbricata, in apicibus ramulorum in cuspidem gemmaceam congesta, late oblonga, ex-cavata, subito in acumen subintegerrimum inferne convolutaceum producta, enervia, cellulis angustis basi ad angulos paucis abbreviatis, perichætialia erecta oblonga sensim subulato-acuminata apicibus erecto-patentibus; theca oblonga, fere sessilis, operculo acuminato, peristomii dentibus subulatis, calyptra ad medium operculi descendens, pilosa, basi integra.—Viti (Amer. Expl. Exped.), abundant on trees in the mountains (Milne! in Herb Hooker), Samoa, Tutuila, on Cocoa-nut, Hibiscus, and other trees, 1000–2000 ft. (Powell! n. 7).

Primary stem tough, creeping over the bark and branches of trees, when old leafless, from this arise numerous erect or ascending branches from 2 to 4 inches high, usually undivided for the space of half or three-quarters of an inch, above this they are regularly pinnate with the length of the branches decreasing towards their apices, or they are more or less closely set with irregular long and short branches in a suffruticose manner, a few stems have been seen which appear to have grown procumbent, and are somewhat elongated, but these do not show a tendency to become pendulous

XIV. **Meteorium,** Brid. Rami fertiles breviusculi, simplices vel pinnatim ramosi, e caule repente vel libero pendulo prolixe continuato oriundi. Folia undique aequalia vel subcompressa, theca immersa vel exserta Peristomium perfectum vel saepius internum ciliis carens. Calyptra plurifida vel dimidiata.

The following species have not yet been found in Viti, viz..—1. *M. aeruginosum*, Mitt. Linn. Soc Journ vol. x p 171 t. 5 B—Samoa, Upolu, on trees (1000–2000 ft), (Powell! n 88). 2. *M. (Eumeteorium) vulcanicum*, (sp. nov) Mitt., rami ramulis curvatis pinnatim ramosi, folia laxe imbricata, oblonga, obtusissima, excavata, apiculo parvo angusto terminata, margine superne involuta, basi subcordata, cellulis ad angulos in maculam fuscam condensatis, superioribus angustis brevibus, ramulina conformia apiculo breviore—Hawaii ad montem iguivomem (Macrae! in Herb Musaei Brit.)—In size and appearance nearly resembling *M molle*, Hedw, but more rigid, and with its leaves tipped with an apiculus. 3 *M. trichophorum*, Mont Ann des Sc Nat 1843, vol xix p. 238 (*Isothecium?*); C Mueller, Syn vol. ii p. 130 (*Neckera*) —Sandwich Islands, on the bark of trees (Gaudichaud!). 4. *M Hornschuchii*, Mitt. Linn. Soc Journ. 1859 (*Trachypus*)—Sunday Island, trees on the summit of the mountains (Milne! n. 90), Kermandec Islands, Raoul Island (M'Gillivray!), Pacific Islands (Beechey!) 5 *M helictophyllum*, Mont. Voy. au Pole Sud (*Cryphaea*)—Tahiti (Lesson, Jaquinot), Pacific Islands (Beechey!). 6. *M. lanosum*, Mitt. Journ of the Proceed Linn Soc 1859 (*M. longissimum*, Dozy et Molk Bryol. Javan. t. 202)—Pacific Islands (Beechey), Samoa, Tutuila, on trees in a damp place (1000–1500 ft) (Powell, n 4). 7. *M. (Aerobryum) striatulum* (sp nov), Mitt; rami elongati, flexuosi, ramulis divergentibus pinnati; folia compressa, late ovato-lanceolata, acuminata, serrulata, nervo angustissimo medio evanido, cellulis angustis papillosis areolata, humida laevia, sicca longitudinaliter quater plicata—Aneitum, in damp places (Milne!), South Sea Islands (Nightingale!)—Stems a foot or more long, slender, soft; foliage more close than in *A lanosum*, and less glossy, ochraceous Very similar to *A. lanosum*, but with a different appearance from the folds in the leaf when dry.

1. **M. intricatum,** Mitt. Linn. Soc. Journ vol x. p. 171. t 5 A; dioicum; rami graciles, elongati, flexuosi, ramulis divergentibus curvatis laxe pinnatim ramosi; folia ramea undique erecto-patentia, torta, a basi cordata, auriculis crenatis, ovato-lanceolata, sensim acuminata, integerrima, nervo obsoleto, cellulis angustis elongatis brevissime obscureque pluripapillatis; folia ramulina superne latiora, haud acuminata, subserrulata, semitorta, medio inferne canaliculata, nervo tenui infra medium obsoleto; folia perichaetialia patentia, longe acuminata, vaginula filis exsertis barbata, pedunculus crassiusculus, sublaevis, foliis perichaetialibus subduplo longior, curvatus; theca oblongo-cylindracea, inaequalis, operculo subulato; peristomium dentibus elongatis irregularibus nonnullis inter se cohaerentibus fissis obscuris, internum processibus angustis obscuris brevioribus, membrana basilari carens, calyptra inferne pilis paucis barbata. Flos masculus parvus, antheridia 8–10 paraphysibus paucis immixta fovens—Viti (Seemann!). Also in Samoa, Tutuila, on living trees in the shady forests (20–1000 ft) (Powell! n. 5).

Foliage green, dark brown in age. In size, colour, and habit, this species agrees with *M. helictophyllum;* but its longer capsule is exserted, and thus it comes nearer to *M floribundum*, Dozy et Molk Musc Archip Ind. t 53, but from this it differs in the cordate-auriculate base of its leaves, and also in the teeth of the external peristome not being united on a base that is exserted above the mouth of the capsule.

2. **M. Vitianum,** Sull. Amer. Expl. Exped. t. 21; majusculum, caulibus longissimis pendulis

divisis rectangulate ramosis, ramis distantibus simplicibus vel pauciramulosis; foliis horizontalibus laxis bifariis e basi lata cordato-ovata lanceolatis filiformi-attenuatis, toto ambitu serratis semicostatis plicato et ruguloso implanis, cellulis minutissimis lineari-fusiformibus unipapillosis.—Viti, on trees (Amer. Expl. Exped.).

Leaves horizontal, loose, bifarious; texture thin and firm (Sull. l c).

XV. **Garovaglia**, Endlich. Caules erecti, simplices vel ramosi, basi tantum radicantes. Folia subbinervia. Theca immersa vel breviter exserta. Peristomium sæpius imperfectum. Calyptra parva.—*Esenbeckia*, Brid. ii. p. 753. *Endotrichum*, Dozy et Molk. Musc. Archip. Ind.

The following species have not yet been found in Viti, viz —1 *G. Powellii*, Mitt. Journ of the Proceed. Linn Soc. 1868, p. 169 —Samoa, Tutuila, on living trees near Letaumata (1000 ft) (Powell! n 3). 2 *G. cuspidata*, Mitt Hooker's Journ. of Bot. 1856, p. 263 —New Caledonia (Vieillard) Also in Australia, Moreton Bay (F. Mueller!). 3. *G. Samoana*, Mitt. Linn Soc. Journ. vol x p. 169 —Samoa, Matie, and Tutuila, near Letaumata (1000 ft) (Powell! n. 70) 4 *G angustifolia*, Mitt. Journ of the Proceed. Linn. Soc. 1868, p. 170.—Pacific Islands (Nightingale! Herb. Hooker).

I. **G. setigera**, Sull. Amer. Expl. Exped. t. 18 B (*Endotrichum*); caulis ascendens, simplex vel ramis paucis divisus, foliis densis imbricatis crassus; folia caulina late oblongo-ovata obtusa cuspidata quater plicata margine apicem versus crenulata, nervis fere obsoletis, cellulis parvis angustis quasi in seriebus transversalibus dispositis, perichætia inter folia caulina semi-immersa, foliis interioribus oblongis convolutis basi breviter binerviis superne in acumen aristiforme serrulatum nervatum elongatum productis; theca immersa, oblonga, basi abrupte in pedunculo brevissimo constricta, operculo cupulato, rostro subulato; peristomii dentes crassi, intus valde trabeculati, interni processus angusti, carinati, in membrana usque ad ¼ dentium longitudinis exserta impositi, calyptra conica, acuminata, plurifida —Viti (Amer. Expl. Exped.), Ovalau (Milne! Seemann! n 846), Samoa, Tutuila (Powell!).

Stems from 2–6 inches high. Foliage straw-coloured, shining

XVI. **Phyllogonium**, Brid. Rami fertiles elongati, pinnati. Folia disticha, complicata, equitantia. Theca immersa vel breviter exserta, peristomio parvo depresso simplici externo. Calyptra parva, dimidiata.

A small genus, of which, besides the Polynesian species, one is found in the Island of Bourbon and in tropical America, and another occurs in New Zealand as well as in Ceylon; the remainder are all South American.

1 **P. angustifolium**, Schimp. in Herb. Mitten; dioicum; rami ramulis remotis inæquilongis pinnati; folia lateralia patentia æqualiter complicata apice excavata apiculo brevissimo recurvo, nonnulla interjecta inæqualiter complicata vel usque ad apicem fere planis, omnia integerrima enervia, cellulis angustis basalibus paucis areolata, perichætia elongata foliis externis parvis ovatis acuminatis patulis recurvis reliquis erectis lanceolatis acuminatis 2–3-plicatis, nervo infra apicem subserrulatum evanido vel breviore; theca immersa, subsessilis, elongata, cylindracea, operculo conico acuminato, peristomio dentibus irregularibus aurantiacis, calyptra parva anguste conica, basi filis paucis brevibus articulatis pilosa.—Viti (Milne!). Also in Nukahiva (Le Bâtard), and Samoa, Tutuila (Powell!).

A bright green, irregularly-branched species, in its immersed capsule allied only to the South American *P. immersum*, Mitt.

XVII. **Neckera**, Hedw. Fund. vol. ii. p. 93. Rami fertiles per longitudinem æqualiter pinnatim ramosi vel basi substipitati. Folia compressa. Theca in perichætio ampliato immersa vel breviter exserta. Peristomium imperfectum. Calyptra parva, plurifida vel dimidiata.

The following two species have not yet been met with in Viti, viz.—1. *N.* (*Teniocladium*, Mitt. Linn. Soc. Journ. vol. x. p. 168) *gracilenta*, Van den Bosch et Lacoste, Bryol. Javan. t. 182.—Samoa, Tutuila (Powell! n. 95). 2. *N. implana*, Mitt. Journ. of the Proceed. Linn. Soc. 1868, p. 169.—Samoa, Tutuila, on trees near Letaumata (1000 feet) (Powell! n. 31).—This species has its leaves more flattened and a little wider than in *N. loriformis*.

1. N. Lepineana, Mont. Ann. des Sc. Nat. 1818, p. 107; Bryol. Javan. t. 181.—Tahiti, Lepine (Beechey), Viti Levu (Milne! n. 337, Seemann! n. 863). Samoa, Tutuila, on trees; in fruit near Lanutoo, the Mountain Lake, Upolu (2500 feet) (Powell! n. 2).

2. N. loriformis, Van den Bosch et Lacoste, Bryol. Javan. t. 183; rami stipitati, superne in frondem ramulis paucis inordinatis ramosi; folia in stipite sparsa, ligulata, in medio frondis a basi latiora, ligulata, patentia divergentiave, compressa, distichacea, subundulata, fere lævia, nervo fere ad apicem obtusum angulatum breviter mucronatum crenulatum continuo, cellulis obscuris superioribus rotundis inferioribus elongatis.—Gau (Milne!), Viti Levu (Seemann! n. 836), Samoa, Tutuila (Powell! n. 118).

Foliage less shining than in *N. implana*, having a rather glaucous appearance. Branches not so rigid, more curved, and attenuated.

XVIII. Porotrichum, Brid. Rami fertiles, inferne simplices stipitiformes, superne in frondem arbusculosam pinnatim divisi. Folia teretiuscule imbricata vel compressa. Theca plus minus longe pedunculata, peristomio perfecto vel interno ciliis carente. Calyptra parva, dimidiata.

The following species have not yet been found in Viti, viz.—1. *P. elegantissimum*, Mitt. Linn. Soc. Journ. vol. x. p. 187, from Samoan Islands, Tutuila, on trees near Letaumata and elsewhere (1000 feet) (Powell! n. 33.) 2. *P. mucronatum*, Van den Bosch et Lacoste, Bryol. Javan. t. 187, from Samoa, Tutuila, on the bark of trees (1000 feet) (Powell! n. 119). 3. *P. Aneitense* (sp. nov.), Mitt., dioicum?; stipes 1–1½-uncialis, foliis parvis ovato-lanceolatis patulis sparsis obtectus, superne in frondem horizontalem ramis abbreviatis divisus, folia ramea subcompressa, imbricata, ovato-oblonga, obtuse acuta, nervo sub apice desinente lævi, margine superne crenulata, cellulis omnibus parvis rotundatis areolata.—Aneitum (Milne! in Herb. Hooker, 369).—Habit that of *P. arcuatum*, Mitt., of India, but smaller, with shorter and firmer leaves, in its size more nearly related to *P. pandum*, Hook. f. et Wils. Fl. N. Zealand, t. 89 f. 1, but with more obtuse leaves, with the nerve not continued to the apex.

1. P. dendroides, Hook. Musc. Exot. t. 69 (*Neckera*). Rami elongati, inferne stipite foliis imbricatis appressis obtecto, superne in frondem pinnatam vel flabellatam bipinnatamque decompositi; folia arcte compressa, patentia, oblonga, parum inæquilatera, acuta, subundulata vel lævia, apice dentata, nervo medio evanescente, cellulis superioribus minutis ovalibus; folia ramea breviora ovalia apiculata, perichætialia parva apicibus loriformi-acuminatis patulis; theca ovalis, brevi-pedunculata.—Viti (Seemann!). Also in Hawaii (Menzies! Douglas!).

A large species with flattened foliage. It is allied to *P. dendroides*, Hornsch. et Reinwardt, from Java (*Neckera Javanica*, C. Müller), and to numerous Indian species, more particularly *P. flabellatum*, Sm. (*Hookeria*), in all which the capsule is borne on a very short fruitstalk on the under side of the fronds.

TRIBUS VIII. SEMATOPHYLLEÆ.—Fructus in ramulo brevissimo e latere caulis vel ramorum oriundo sæpius longe pedunculatus. Folia enervia vel rarissime breviter binervia, cellulis basalibus ad angulos paucis oblongis a reliquis sæpe colore diversis.

The following have been found out of Viti.—I. MEIOTHECIUM: 1, *M. stratosum*, Mitt., from Samoa, Tutuila (Powell! 27), 2, *M. intextum*, Mitt., from Samoa, Manua, on Breadfruit-trees (500 feet) (Powell! 42), 3, *M. microcarpum*, Harvey in Hook. Icon. Plant. Rar. t. 24 f. 12 (*Pterogonium*), from Samoa, Tutuila, on Orange-trees (Powell! n. 36). II. TAXITHELIUM: 1, *T. Samoanum*, Mitt. Linn. Soc. Journ. v. x. from Samoa, Upolu, on trees (2000 feet) (Powell! n. 132), 2, *T. tenuisetum*, Sull. Proceed. Amer. Acad. of Arts and Sc. vol. iii., from Samoa, Tutuila, American Expedition (Powell!), South Sea Islands (Nightingale!).

[PUBLISHED JUNE 1, 1871.] 3 F

XIX. **Sematophyllum,** Mitt Caulis procumbens repensve, pinnatim ramosus Fructus c caule vel c ramis oriundus. Theca oblonga, inclinata, operculo longo subulato, peristomio interno processibus in membrana impositis, ciliis nullis vel imperfectis

An extensive genus of Mosses, with nearly always nerveless leaves, in which the alar cells at the angles of the leaf are enlarged, and of a different colour from those immediately above them. The species not yet found in Viti are —1, *S. brevicuspidatum*, Mitt Linn Soc Journ. vol x p 183, from Samoa, Manua, on large trees (1500 feet) (Powell n 137), Sandwich Islands and South Sea Islands (Herb. Hooker), 2, *S. macrorhynchum*, Mitt Linn Soc Journ vol x 1868, p 183, from Samoa, Manua, on large trees in moist places (2000 feet) (Powell n 115), 3, *S turgidum*, Dozy et Molk., C. Mueller, Syn. vol ii p 396 (*Hypnum*), from Samoa, Tutuila (Powell); 4, *S. stigmosum*, Mitt Journ of the Proceed Linn Soc 1868, p 181, from Samoa, Upolu, Matafao (1000 feet) (Powell n. 21), 5, *S lamprophyllum*, Mitt. Journ of the Proceed Linn Soc 1868, p 183, from Samoa, Upolu, on trees (1000 feet) (Powell n 114), 6, *S fissum*, Mitt Journ of the Proceed Linn Soc 1868, p 182, from Samoa, Upolu, on trees (Powell n 116), 7, *S. opæodon*, Sull Amer Expl Exped t 11 B, from Sandwich Islands (Douglas), 8, *S contiguum*, Hook. f et Wils., from Lord Howe's Island (Milne!), Isle of Pines (Strange! M'Gillivray l), St Paul's Island (Strange)

1. **S. rigidum,** Nees et Reinw. (*Hypnum*), Bryol Javan t. 238; dioicum; caulis procumbens, arcuatus, apice radicans, inde prolifero continuatus erectus vel ascendens, arcuatus, arbusculoso-ramosus; folia patentia in cauli primario late ovalia subito in acumen subulatum denticulatum producta in ramis assurgentibus late ovato-lanceolata superne denticulata, ramulina elliptico-lanceolata margine incurva serrata, omnia cellulis angustis alaribus conspicuis flavis, perichætialia erecta acumine elongato loriformi dentato; theca in pedunculo longissimo ovalis, horizontalis, operculo conico acuminato —*Hypnum Calderense*, Sull. Amer. Exped. t. 15?—Viti Levu (Milne!). Also in Isle of Pines (Strange!), Samoa, Tutuila (Powell! n. 55), Aneitum (Milne!).

A very large and handsome species, which occurs also in Java.

2. **S. papillatum,** Harvey in Lond. Journ. of Bot. 1810; Hook Icon. Plant. Rar. i t 23 f. 8 (*Hypnum*); dioicum; caulis procumbens, arcuatus, ramulis pluribus breviusculis; folia caulina patentia ovata in acumen elongatum subulatum producta, ramea ovata subulato-acuminata, omnia concava margine serrulata, cellulis angustis dorso dense papillosis alaribus distinctis flavis, perichætialia longiora longe subulata serrulata; theca longissime tenui-pedunculata, parva, oblonga, horizontalis, demum curvata, operculo conico acuminato, peristomio interno, ciliis in uno coalitis.—Ovalau, on stumps of trees in high ground, frequent (Milne!). Also Samoa, Tutuila (Powell, n. 25).

Far less in all its parts than *S rigidum*, and, like it, found also in Java, as well as in Borneo and the Malayan Peninsula It appears to grow in very extensive loosely-matted patches, spreading over decayed wood

3. **S. Borbonicum,** Bel. Voy. Crypt. t. 11. f. 2 (*Leskea*); monoicum, depresse cæspitosum, ramis ascendentibus decurvis, folia compressa secunda curvata anguste elongate lanceolata concava serrulata, cellulis elongatis quadripapillatis alaribus magnis hyalinis, perichætialia erecta subulato-attenuata serrulata; pedunculus minute scabrosus; theca parva, oblonga, horizontalis, operculo tenui longirostro.—*Hypnum Pickeringii*, Sull. Amer. Expl. Exped. t. 15 A —Viti (Milne!, Seemann!). Also Solomon Islands (Milne), Samoa, Tutuila (Powell! n. 117), Isle of Pines (Strange!).

TRIBUS IX. **STEREODONTEÆ.**—Fructus in ramulo brevissimo laterali sæpius longe pedunculatus Folia binervia vel enervia, cellulis basilaribus ad angulos sæpe abbreviatis densioribus.

The following members of this tribe have not yet been found in Viti —1 ENTODON, C Mull 1 *E pallidus* (sp nov), Mitt , monoicus, rami procumbentes, pinnati, folia compressa late ovata acuta subacuminatave brevissime binervia margine subserrulata, cellulis angustis ad angulos basalibus pluribus abbreviatis quadratis, ramulina compressa ovali-elliptica acuta apice subserrulata, perichætialia erecta basi ovata inde subulata apice recurva, theca in pedunculo elongato stramineo cylindracea, peristomio interno processibus rubris dentium externe æquilongis.—New Ireland (Labillardière), Tahiti (Menzies), Lord Howe's Island (Milne! M'Gillivray!), Isle of Pines (Milne!), St Paul's Island (Strange!), Aneitum (Milne!).— Less compressed than the Indian and Javan *E. plicatus*, C. Muller, with wider leaves. II. CYRTOPUS, Schimp. 1. *C. stellulatum* (sp nov), Mitt., caulis ramulis brevibus pinnatus; folia patenti-divergentia, a basi subcordato-ovata, sensim longe subulato-attenuata, obsoletinervia, margine ubique serrulata, cellulis angustis areolata, ramea compressa lanceolato-subulata argutius serrulata.—Society Islands (Bidwill!)— Stems one to two inches long. Foliage greenish-yellow, glossy, arranged at the apices of the stems in a stellate manner. III. STEREODON, Brid. 1, *S Draytoni*, Sull. Proceed. Amer. Acad. of Arts and Sc. 1851, from Hawaii, forest at the eastern base of Manua Kea (American Expedition!), 2, *S Eudora*, Sull. Proceed Amer Acad of Arts and Sc. 1851, from Oahu and Hawaii (American Expedition!); 3, *S decurrens*, Sull. Proceed. Amer. Acad of Arts and Sc 1851, from Sandwich Islands, Oahu, and Hawaii Mountains (American Expedition). IV. PTYCHOMNION, Hook f. et Wils. 1. *P. aciculare*, Brid. Musc Rec vol ii. p 2, 158 t 5 f 2 (*Hypnum*), from Samoa, Manua, on trees (Powell! n. 105), Norfolk Island (Cunningham!).—Abundant in New Zealand and Tasmania, also in Australia and the western coast of South America

XX. Leucomium, Mitt. Linn. Soc. Journ vol v. Caulis procumbens, subsimplex vel pinnatus. Folia compressa, æqualia, enervia, laxissime areolata. Theca parva, horizontalis pendulave, operculo longirostri; peristomii externi dentes lamina exteriore integra vel divisa, interni ciliis plus minus perfectis nullisve.

A small genus, consisting chiefly of tropical American species; all have their leaves very laxly areolate, and the stems attached to decaying wood or to rotten leaves.

1. **L. debile,** Sull. Amer. Expl. Exped p. 23. t. 21 (*Hookeria*); monoicum et synoicum; caulis ramis paucis irregularibus ramosus; folia compressa lateralia patentia, omnia ovato-lanceolata subulato-attenuata integerrima enervia, cellulis amplis pellucidis areolata, perichætialia parva erecta vel erecto-patentia ovata acuminata; theca in pedunculo gracillimo rubro ovalis, horizontalis, collo sensim attenuato, operculo subulirostrato; peristomium internum ciliis carentibus.—Gau, on decayed trees (Milne! n. 22), Samoan Islands, Tutuila (Powell! n. 24).

Pale green, and when older pale whitish-brown and glossy, the leaves are not much altered in direction when dry.

XXI. Isopterygium, Mitt Linn. Soc. Journ 1868. Caulis procumbens, ramis inæquilongis fasciculatim ramosis. Folia compressa, disticha, seriebus tribus superioribus (centrali intermediisque) vix obviis, seriebus tribus inferioribus deficientibus, brevissime binervia, cellulis angustis lævibus. Theca inclinata horizontalisve, oblonga, ciliis peristomii interni coalitis.

A group of mostly very small Mosses, with compressed, almost distichous leaves.

1. **I. molliculum,** Sull. Amer. Expl. Exped. t. 11 (*Hypnum*), monoicum, caulis decumbens, parce ramosus; folia compressa distichacea ovato-lanceolata acuminata integerrima enervia, cellulis angustis elongatis, perichætialia longius acuminata; theca in pedunculo elongato ovalis, subhorizontalis, operculo acuminato.—Viti (Milne!). Also in Lord Howe's Island, on rotten wood (Milne and M'Gillivray!), and Raoul Island, Kermandec Islands (M'Gillivray!).

A minute species, softer than the tropical American *I tenerum*, Sw (*Hypnum*).

XXII. Ectropothecium, Mitt. Linn. Soc. Journ. vol. v. p. 10. Caulis procumbens, ramis brevibus æqualibus dense pinnatus. Folia compressa, diversiformia, breviter binervia, cellulis angustis latisve areolata. Fructus e caule oriundus. Theca in pedunculo elongato, brevis, horizontalis vel pendula, urceolata, operculo brevirostri, peristomii interni ciliis coalitis.

A genus of numerous species, all of which are elegantly branched and prostrate. The foliage is most

3 Y 2

frequently secund, the leaves on the upper side of the stem larger than on the under, and usually of a different form The areolation is either (as in Sp 1–6) with elongate, narrow, close-placed cells, or in some species (7–8) very lax and pellucid 1, *E pacificum*, Mitt Journ of the Proceed Linn Soc 1868, p. 180, from Samoa, without fruit (Powell!), Tobie Island, also in Eromanga (Bennett! Herb Hooker), 2, *E sodale*, Sull Amer Expl Exped t. 12 f B (*Hypnum*) (*Hypnum molluscoides*, Sull. Proceed Amer. Acad. of Arts and Sc 1853, e notula ejusd. in Amer Expl Exped p 15), from Society Islands (Eimeo! American Expedition), Tahiti (Beechey!), South Sea Islands (Nightingale!), Samoa, Tutuila (Powell!), 3, *E Sandwichense*, Hook. et Arn Botany of Beechey Voy. p 109 (*Hypnum*), from Oahu, Sandwich Islands (Lay et Collie! Beechey!), Sunday Island (Milne!), Samoa, Tutuila (Powell!), 4, *E arcuatum*, Sull. Proceed Amer. Acad of Arts and Sc 1854, from Sandwich Islands, East Maui (American Expedition); 5, *E. gracilisetum*, Hornsch et Reinw. Schw t 220, from Hawaii, District of Puna (American Expedition); 6, *E fuscescens*, Hook et Arnott in Beechey Voy t 19 (*Hypnum*), from Tahiti (Beechey!), Samoa, Tutuila, on stones and rocks in gullies and streams where the flow of water is frequent (Powell! n. 20), 7, *E inflectens*, Brid vol ii p 331, from Tahiti (Dumont et D'Urville), Samoa, Tutuila (Powell?)

1. **E. Tutuilum**, Sull. Amer. Expl. Exped t 10 f. A (*Hypnum*), dioicum?; caules prostrati, pinnati; folia compressa subsecunda media sublanceolata planiuscula lateralia inæquilatera curvata subcomplicata omnia nervis brevissimis, margine e medio ad apicem usque crebre serrulata, cellulis angustis, perichætialia basi late ovalia erecta inde in subulam angustam serrulatam patulam producta; theca in pedunculo elongato breviter ovalis, demum pendula, operculo conico acuminato—Viti (Milne!). Also in Samoa, Tutuila (American Expedition, Powell!).

Stems two or three inches long, with branches two to three lines in length. Foliage almost shining, greenish, becoming straw-coloured and brownish

TRIBUS X. **HYPNEÆ**—Fructus in ramulo brevissimo sæpius longe pedunculatus. Folia uninervia.

The following members of this tribe have not yet been found in Viti, viz :—I HYPNUM, L. Caulis procumbens repensive, ramis pinnatim dispositis vel ascendentibus in cæspitem congestis, interdum ascendens suberectus subarbusculosus. Folia undique æqualia, cellulis elongatis areolata. Theca erecta inclinata horizontalisve, æqualis vel gibba—A very extensive genus of Mosses, divisible into some sections, which are more easily seen than exactly capable of definition Nearly all the Polynesian specimens belong to the group named by Schimper *Rhynchostegium*, the capsules having a long beaked operculum 1. *H compressifolium* (sp nov.), Mitt; synoicum, caulis decumbens, ramis irregularibus subpinnatim divisus; folia compressa ovato-ovalia acuminata planiuscula, nervo ultra medium producto, margine serrulata, cellulis angustis elongatis, ramea ulteriora ovalia acuta distinctius serrulata, perichætialia subulata attenuata; pedunculus elongatus, ubique tenuissime scabrosus, theca ovalis, inæqualis, horizontalis, operculo subulirostrato.—Sunday Island (Milne! n. 91), Raoul Island, Kermandec Islands (M'Gillivray!)—This species, in size and appearance, nearly resembles the *Hypnum tenuifolium*, Hedw, so frequent in Australia, Tasmania, and New Zealand, and it is allied to *H austrinum*, H f et W, but differs in habit in the more strongly-nerved and more compressed foliage In these particulars it differs also from the New Zealand *H. asperipes*, Mitt, which has more cordate not compressed leaves. Fragments of a different species were collected in Samoa by Powell 2. *H. Wilkesianum*, Sull. Proceed of the Amer. Acad. of Arts and Sc 1854—Hawaii (American Expedition) II SCIAROMIUM, Mitt Caulis primarius repens, ramos arbusculosos vel vage elongatos producens. Folia æqualia, cellulis parvis brevibus obscuris densis Theca inclinata horizontalisve—A group of species mostly of large size, with rigid stems and firm foliage, which is of a dull, obscure green colour In some particulars this genus approaches some species of *Porothrichum* or *Thamnium*. 1. *S glauco-viride*, Mitt., rami inferne stipitati, superne ramulis sparsis pinnatim ramosi, elongati, folia patentia firma setacea n basi subovato-lanceolata biplicata sensim longe angustata, nervo percurrente usque ad apicem a pagina folii planiuscula distincto, cellulis minutis obscuris rotundis, perichætialia basi ovalia tenera inde longe subulata patula, pedunculus elongatus, ruber, theca oblonga, horizontalis, operculo subulato—Sunday Island, trees on the summit of the mountains frequent (Milne! n 91), Norfolk Island—Dull glaucous-green Closely resembling the *Hypnum hispidum* figured in Plate LXI F 2, of the 'Flora Antarctica,' but a little more slender, and the points of the foliage more narrow. 2 *S tricostatum*, Sull Proceed Amer Acad of Arts and Sc vol iii. (*Neckera*), Amer. Expl Exped, cum icone—Hawaii, forest at the eastern base of Mauna Kea (Amer. Exped), Oahu and Hawaii ad Mont Kaah (Macrae! in Herb Mus Brit) III PTEROKIUM, Mitt Journ. of the Proceed Linn Soc 1868, p. 176; caulis procumbens, bipinnatim ramosus, phyllodiis vestitus, folia uninervia, cellulis rotundatis papillosis areolata, fructus lateralis, theca longe pedunculata, peristomium normale; calyptra magna, plicata, basi multifida. 1. *P. relatum*, Mitt l. c.—Samoa, Tutuila, on damp stones and decayed logs in woods and other shady places (10-50 feet) (Powell! n. 14). Found also in Borneo and Java (Motley!).

XXIII. **Hypnodendron**, C. Muller. Caulis primarius repens, rhizomatiformis, ramos erectos inferne simplices superne in frondem decompositos producens. Folia in media fronde æqualia vel inæqualia et compressa. Theca inclinata horizontalisve, plicata, peristomio perfecto.

A small genus of large and handsome species, conspicuous for their tree-like growth, of which the following have not yet been found in Viti, viz.—1. *H. rigidum*, (sp nov.), Mitt., ramus erectus, inferne simplex, foliis appressis tenuiter acuminatis obtectus, demum denudatus, rigidus, superne in frondem suboblongam ramis simplicibus ramulosisve pluribus pinnatus, folia in frondis medio late subovata lanceolata, acuta, substriata, nervo percurrente dorso dentato, margine serrulata, cellulis angustissimis densis firmis areolata—Aneitum (Milne!)—Fronds with the stipes four inches high. Foliage dull brownish-green. 2 *H. Samoanum*, Mitt. Journ of the Proceed Linn Soc 1868, p 192.—Samoa, Tutuila, on trees and rocks in the beds of gullies (100-2000 feet) (Powell! n 107). 3. *H. Milnei* (sp nov.), Mitt, stipes bi-triuncialis, ruber, rigidus, erectus, apice in comam frondiformem subdeltoideam subhorizontalem divisum; folia in stipite laxe imbricata, patentia, late ovata, acuminata, nervo excurrente, margine serrata, cellulis elongatis ad margines folii minoribus brevioribus, basalibus ad angulos majoribus fuscidulis, folia in ramis ovato-lanceolata nervo excurrente dorso dentato marginibus dentibus duplicatis serrata—Aneitum (Milne!)—Near to *H. divaricatum*, but differing in the stipes not being covered with rootlets, the leaves of the branches shorter, more dense and rigid. In the same respects this species differs from the *H comosum, H. Sieberi*, and *H. comatum* of Australia, Tasmania, and New Zealand. 4 *H divaricatum*, Hornsch. et Reinw. Nova Acta Acad Cæs Leop. 14 vol ii Suppl. t 40—Isle of Pines (Milne!).

1. **H. speciosissimum**, Sull Proceed. Amer. Acad. of Arts and Sc. 1854; Amer. Expl. Exped. t 9 (*Hypnum*), rami stipite elongato rigido denudato, superne in frondem oblongam planam vel ramulis inferioribus nonnullis assurgentibus bipinnatam innovationibus e superiore latere frondis egredientibus proliferi; folia compressa erecto-patentia inferne ovato-lanceolata sensim longe subulato-acuminata rigida plana, nervo percurrente margine superne remote subserrulata, cellulis angustis elongatis densis firmis, folia ramea ramulinaque angustiora argute serrulata, perichætialia erecta; theca in pedunculo breviusculo erecta, ovalis, operculo conico acuminato—Viti (American Expedition). Also in the Malay Archipelago (Herb. Hooker!), and in the Philippine Islands (Cuming! n 2198).

Stipes three inches long, the branched upper portion as long or longer. Foliage firm, unaltered in drying, not glossy, of a red-brown colour

2 **H. Vitiense**, (sp. nov.) Mitt.; folia compressa, ovato-lanceolata, acuta, planiuscula, splendentia, nervo dorso superne denticulato percurrente, marginibus denticulis duplicatis brevibus serratis, cellulis angustis elongatis finitimis prominulis.—Viti (Seemann, n. 842).

H Junghuhniano omnibus partibus primo aspectu simillimum, sed foliis breviter duplicate serrulatis et colore pallidiore

In the list of Vitian species published in 'Bonplandia' this species was mistaken for *H Junghuhnianum*, which it so much resembles

3. **H. arborescens**, Mitt. Journ of the Proceed. Linn. Soc 1859 (*Trachyloma*); rami erecti, inferne stipite foliis sparsis patulis, superne in frondem subovatam lanceolatamve pinnatim bipinnatimve ramosi; folia e medio rami primarii compressa ovato-lanceolata acutissima, nervo excurrente, dorso denticulato, margine denticulis duplicatis serrato, cellulis angustissimis subnodulosis, folia ramulina anguste lanceolata grossius serrata, perichætialia longiora erecta subulata subintegerrima; theca in pedunculo elongato cylindracea, demum plicata inclinata subhorizontalisve, operculo recto sensim acuminato, peristomio dentibus intus valde trabeculatis interno processibus carinatis pertusis

cilusque tribus interpositis in membrana usque ad medium dentium longitudinis exserta impositis — Ovalau (Seemann! n 845, Milne! n 351). Also in Sandwich Islands (Herb. Hooker!), Samoa, Tutuila (Powell! n 111), Ceylon, and in the Malay Archipelago

Foliage green and shining, becoming in age straw-coloured and fulvous.

XXIV. **Thuidium,** Schimp. Caulis procumbens ascendensve, interdum arcuatus, apicibus descendentibus radicantibusque, exinde prolifero-continuatus, paraphyllis obtectus, rarius nudus, ramis ramulisque bipinnatim dispositis bi-tripinnatus. Folia caulina æqualia, ramea ramulinaque diversiformia, inæqualia, cellulis elongatis vel abbreviatis, sæpius papilliferis obscuris. Theca inclinata horizontalisve, rarissime erecta, peristomio perfecto vel ciliis interdum imperfectis obsoletisve.

The following two species have not yet been gathered in Viti, viz —1 *T plicatum* (sp nov), Mitt ; caulis procumbens, irregulariter bipinnatus; folia patentia, cordata, acuminata, plicata, breviuscula, margine inferne reflexa, superne minute crenulata, nervo sub apice evanido, cellulis rotundatis obscuriusculis papillis minutissimis brevissimis, ramea subcompressa patentia cordato-acuminata plicata, ramulina imbricata ovata acuta concava crenulata dorso papillosa, perichætialia a basi lanceolata sensim longe attenuata serrulata ; theca in pedunculo elongato cylindracea inæqualis inclinata —Sandwich Islands (Douglas! in Herb Hooker) —More slender than *T Samoanum*, and less regularly-branched than *T ramentosum*   2 *T. crenulatum* (sp nov), Mitt.; monoicum, caulis bipinnatus, folia patentia cordata subulato-acuminata, nervo sub apice evanido, margine crenulata, inferne subrecurva, cellulis rotundatis obscuriusculis, ramea compressa ramulinaque ovata acuta nervo carinata crenulata, perichætialia longe subulato-attenuata subserrulata, theca in pedunculo elongato ovalis horizontalis, operculo subulato ; peristomium internum ciliis binis inter se cohærentibus trabeculatis —Sandwich Islands (Douglas! in Herb Hooker 57) —Similar to *T. minutulum*, Hedw. Musc Frond 4 t 31

1. T. ramentosum, Mitt in Bonpl. 1861, p 366 (*Leskea*), caulis arcuatus, proliferus, folia caulina a basi lata hastata cauli angustiore subulata, nervo percurrente, margine reflexa integerrima, ramea hastato-ovata acuminata, ramulina ovata incurva papillosa, margine ut in rameis crenulato-serrulata, nervo infra apicem abrupto, dorso prominente cristato, perichætialia interiora in ramentis quamplurimis elongatis flexuosis intricatis serrulatis lacera —Viti (Seemann! inter 863).

Very like the *T cymbifolium,* Dozy et Molk Bry Javan. t 221, from Java and India, but more slender.

2. T. Samoanum, Mitt. Journ. of the Proceed. Linn. Soc. 1868, p 186, caules procumbentes, erecti arcuatique, pinnæformiter bipinnati; folia caulina appressa a basi subtriangulari-ovata sensim in acumen ligulatum obtusiusculum producta lævia, nervo infra apicem evanido, margine crenulato, cellulis rotundis, papillis fere obsoletis, perichætialia interna a basi lata sensim angustata et in acumen elongatum loriforme flexuosum obtusum crenulatum producta, marginibus inferne ciliis pluribus elongatis angustis ciliata; theca in pedunculo elongato cylindracea, arcuata, horizontalis.— Viti (Seemann!). Also Solomon Islands, Guadalcamar (Milne!), Samoan Islands, Tutuila, and Manua, on large stones in gulleys (100–2000 feet) (Powell! 103).

Nearly allied, as so many of the species of this genus are, the present, although externally closely corresponding with *T ramentosum,* is well distinguished by its obtuse cauline leaves

3. T. erosulum, Mitt. Journ. of the Proceed. Linn. Soc. 1868, p. 186; monoicum; caulis repens, intricatus, bipinnatim ramosus; folia patentia triangularia subulato-acuminata, nervo sub apice evanido, marginibus reflexis subintegerrimis, cellulis obscuris, papillis brevissimis; folia ramea ovata acuta, ramulinaque ovata obtusiuscula compressa, nervo pallido dorso scabro carinata, marginibus crenulatis, cellulis papillosis obscuris areolata, perichætialia ovata superne denticulata exinde longe subulata anguste attenuata subintegerrima, nervis percurrentibus; pedunculus elongatus, scaber; theca oblonga, subhorizontalis, operculo subulato; peristomium internum ciliis in unum coalitis.—Island of Wakaya, Viti (Milne!). Also in Samoan Islands, Tutuila, on stones, rocks, and roots of trees in shady places (10–50 feet) (Powell! 29).

In size and mode of growth this agrees nearly with *Pelekium relatum*, but its fruit and calyptra are those of *Thuidium*.

2. **NEMATODONTES.**—*Peristomii dentes e filis liberis vel in processus dentiformes coalitis compositi.*

Tribus XI. **POLYTRICHEÆ.**—Peristomii dentes breves, apicibus ad columellæ apicem in tympani formam expansum adhærentibus.

An extensive tribe of Mosses, with a somewhat creeping, subterraneous rooting stem, from which arise erect, usually simple, very rarely branched, and subdendroid stiff stems, clothed with frequently firm and rigid leaves, scarcely altered in drying; in some species, however, they are soft and curled when dry. The fruit arises from the apex of the stem, and is usually borne on a stout seta. The capsule is either cylindrical and smooth, or more or less strongly angled, even sometimes cubical. The calyptra is almost naked, or more or less completely covered and hidden by appressed hairs

XXV. **Pogonatum,** Brid. Theca cylindracea, lævis vel indistincte plicata. Calyptra indumento villoso obtecta

P. aloides, Hedw., is confined to the Hawaiian Islands (Gaudichaud).

1. **P. Vitiense** (sp. nov.), Mitt ; caulis elongatus, simplex vel innovans; folia subimbricata, a basi latiore erecta pellucida, cellulis inferioribus oblongis, superioribus abbreviatis transverse oblongisque areolata, inde in folium oblongum patenti-incurvum acutum planiusculum intus lamellis brevibus ubique obtectum producta, margine apicem versus denticulis paucis serrulata, perichætialia longiora, a basi erecta longiore latioreque late ovali cæterum caulinis similia; theca in pedunculo elongato, breviter oblonga, inclinata vel horizontalis, scaberrima, 4-carinata; calyptra indumento pallide fulvo appresso, thecam totam obtegens.—Viti (Milne!).

Caulis 1½-3-uncialis. Folia viridia, sicca subnigra. Pedunculus ½-1-uncialis Habitus *P. Teysmanni,* Dozy et Molk similis, foliis autem latioribus —Three or four barren stems of a *Pogonatum* were gathered in Tutuila by Mr Powell, but, although appearing to come very near the species above described, the leaves are narrower and longer.

Tab 97, fig 1. Stems of the natural size, fig 2, a leaf, with transverse section, magnified.

Tribus XII. **BUXBAUMIÆ.**—Peristomium duplex, externum imperfectum vel subobsoletum, internum e membrana conoidea indivisa apice truncata, plicis extus acutis.

XXVI. **Diphyscium,** Mohr. Caulis humilis, interdum fere nullus. Folia ligulata, perichætialia magna diversiformia. Theca magna, subovata, obliqua, ad operculum erectum ascendens.

1. **D. submarginatum,** (sp. nov.) Mitt. ; caulis brevis; folia patentia, spathulato-ligulata, margine cellulis minoribus incrassatis fuscescentioribus sublimbata subdenticulata, cellulis parvis rotundatis obscuriusculis areolata, perichætialia a basi anguste subulata, nervo excurrente sublævi, sensim attenuata.—Viti (Seemann!).

Three plants only, adhering to the rootlets of a specimen of *Thuidium ramentosum.*

B. **HETERODICTYI.**—*Folia cellulis biformibus areolata.*

Tribus XIII **SPHAGNEÆ.**—Caules erecti, simplices vel furcati, ramis simplicibus adscendentibus vel recurvis in fasciculos confertis undique e caule egredientibus vestitus. Folia apice sæpe dissilientia, angustissime limbata, cellulis amplis poris pertusis, sæpius fibro repletis, parietibus e cellulis angustioribus viridibus formatis Fructus ex apice rami proprii e centro fasciculorum oriundus. Theca sessilis, globosa, demum in prolongatione rami fertilis pedunculiformi exserta, operculo convexo; calyptra tenuissima, medio transversim rupta parte inferiore vaginula adhærente obvelata. Flores masculi antheridiis globosis pedicellatis in axillis foliorum, ad apices ramorum amentiformes congesti. Genus unicum :—

XXVII. **Sphagnum,** Dill. Caulis erectus, fastigiato-ramosus, ramis flagelliformibus. Folia caulina pentasticha, ramulina diversiformia densius texta, omnia ecostata. Fructus e ramulis oriundus. Theca globosa, solida, operculo hemisphærico, annulo peristomioque destituta.

S acutifolium, Ehrh , has been found at St. Paul's Island, on the summit of the mountain (Milne! n. 22)

1. **S. cuspidatum,** Ehrh.; caulis plus minus elongatus, fasciculis ramorum remotiusculis, cortice distincto nullo; folia caulina ovata acuta, limbo indistincto, ramea imbricata ovato-lanceolata limbo lato marginata, cellulis majoribus fibro repletis; folia in ramo fertili oblonga ovaliave, cellulis majoribus inanibus.—Viti (Seemann! n. 839).

This species is easily recognized from most of its congeners by the absence of any distinct pellucid cortical cells. The Vitian specimens are without fruit, but have all the appearances of being precisely the same as European.

Ordo CIX. JUNGERMANNIÆ.

(AUCTORE W. MITTEN)

The following genera have not as yet been found in Viti, viz. :—

I. **Conoscyphus,** Mitt. gen. nov. Caulis procumbens ascendensve, ramosus. Folia sursum secunda, integra paucidentatave. Amphigastria magna. Perianthium proprium nullum, e foliis involucralibus in conum convolutis apice dentibus paucis inflexis formatum

1 *C inflexifolius*, (sp. n) Mitt., caulis procumbens, elongatus, parum divisus, folia antice inflexa, subovata, obtusa, margine dorsali sinuata integerrima, ventrali convexa, caulem versus bidentata, amphigastria magna rotunda, apice bidentata, lateribus tridenticulatis, folia involucralia teretiusculo imbricata.—Samoa, inter cæspites *Syrrhopodontis crocei, Sendtnerœ juniperinæque*, sparsim crescens (Powell) —Rami 2 uncias longi, cum foliis lineam lati Folia castaneo-fusca, imbricata —Similar in habit, colour, and appearance to *Lophocolea devexa*, Mitt. Journ. of the Linn Soc vol vii p 165, and to the *Chiloscyphus trapezoides* and *C Tjicideensis*, Van der Sande Lacoste, Hep Javan t 7, all probably belong to the same genus The Samoan specimens have the inner involucral leaves convolute, so as to form a flask-like perianth, but they do not appear to be anywhere combined with each other or with the stipule, at their bases they are adherent to the lower part of the calyptra. In *C. devexus* the involucral leaves are arranged in a similar manner; but as only young states of the fructification were present, it was supposed that the species was allied to some austral South American species of *Lophocolea*, as *L Gayana* (*Chiloscyphus*), Mont , the fructification being evidently terminal, but supposed to be incomplete The occurrence, however, of the same kind of involucre with young capsules leaves no doubt but that a true and tubular perianth is wanting in both the African and Samoan species The place of this genus is somewhat obscure In habit, and in the substance of its leaves and its conspicuous stipules, it corresponds most nearly with some species of *Lophocolea* and of *Leioscyphus*

II. **Lophocolea,** Nees ab E , Gottsche, Lindenb et Nees Syn. Hepat. p 151.

1. *L Gaudichaudi*, Mont. Voy de la Bonite, Bot. Crypt t. 148. f 4 —Sandwich Islands (Gaudichaud, Hillebrand!).

2 *L Beecheyana*, Tayl. Lond Journ of Bot. 1846, p. 365 —Hawaii (Beechey!).

3 *L explanata* (sp nov), Mitt , caulis repens, ramosus, folia explanata, convexa, ovata, apice sinu parvo excisa, basi cum amphigastrio parvo bifido, segmentis extus unidentatis, anguste coalita vel libera, involucralia ovalia, margine ubique ciliata, perianthium angulis alatum, ala anteriore latiore, lateralibus labiisque dentato-ciliatis —Samoa (Powell!) —Caulis unciam longus, cum foliis lineam latus. Folia pallida, tenera

4. *L rectangulata* (sp nov), Mitt , caulis procumbens, elongatus, folia explanata, plana, oblonga, subrectangulata, apice abrupta bidentata, margine ventrali cum amphigastrio tridentato, laciniis utroque uni-

dentatis coalito —Samoa (Powell!)—Caulis 1-2 uncias longus, cum foliis 1½ lineam latus Folia tenera, fusca

5 *L convexula* (sp. nov), Mitt.; caulis brevis, radicans infra perianthium innovans, folia explanata, imbricata, convexa, ovata, apice sinu parvo obtuso obtuse bidentata, rarius integra, rotundata, amphigastria parva, bifida, lacinus unidentatis, basi libera; folia involucralia majora, flabelliformia, amphigastrioque magno grosse dentata —Isle of Pines (Strange!)—Caulis 3-6 lineas longus, cum foliis semilineam latus Folia pallide albo-viridia, crassiuscula

6 *L spinosa*, Gottsch., idem Ldbg. et Nees Syn. Hep p 170 —Hawaii, inter *Lejeuniam* occulatum legit Gottsche.

III CHANDONANTHUS. Mitt in Hooker, 'Handbook of the New Zealand Flora,' vol ii p 753
1 *C hirtellus*, Web Prod p. 50 (*Jungermannia*).—Pacific Islands (Herb Hooker!).

IV. PLECTOCOLEA, Mitt Linn Soc Journ vol viii p 156
1. *P. micrantha* (sp nov), Mitt; caulis humilis, radiculosus; folia ovali-rotunda, patentia, semi-verticalia, involucralia majora, margine dorsali recurva; perianthium parvum, elongato-ovatum, apice ultra folia involucralia non productum—Sandwich Islands (Hillebrand!)—Caulis 2-3 lineas altus Folia ½ lineam longa, involucralia lineam metientes viridia. Perianthium lineam brevius —Larger than the Indian *P. polyrhiza*, Hook, but agreeing with it and with *P Junghuhniana* and *P Hasskarliana*, Nees ab E (*Jungermannia*), both found in Java, in the perianth, which is plicated throughout its length, and not contracted at its apex into a tubular mouth, thus differing from *Jungermannia* as here considered, in which the terminal perianth is teretе below, plicate towards the apex, and the mouth contracted and dentato-ciliate.

V SPHAGNOECETIS, Nees ab E, Gottsche, Lindenb et Nees Syn Hepat. 118
1 *S gracilis* (sp nov), Mitt, caulis elongatus, parce radiculosus; folia explanata, orbiculata, cellulis interstitiis latioribus pellucidis discretis areolata, amphigastria obsoleta —Ins Sandwich (Gaudichaud) —Caulis unciam brevior, cum foliis ¼ lineam latus—Similar in habit to *S. communis*, but less, with almost round leaves, and the marginal cells, instead of being prominent as in that species, are smaller, and less easily definable than those of the interior of the leaf

VI GOTTSCHEA, Nees ab E; Gottsche, Lindenb et Nees Syn Hepat 13
1. *G aligera*, Nees ab E Hep Javan p 67; Gottsche, Lindenb. et Nees Syn. Hepat p. 17.—Pacific Islands (Nightingale! in Herb Hooker, n 288), Samoa (Powell! n. 75)

VII TRICHOCOLEA, Dumort; Gottsche, Lindenb. et Nees Syn. Hepat. p. 236
1 *T tomentella*, Ehrh —Samoa (Powell!)

VIII. SENDTNERA, Endlicher, Gen p. 1312.
1 *S juniperina*, Swartz, Fl Ind. Occid 1855 (*Jungermannia*) —Samoa (Powell! n 142), Hawaii, (Douglas! Tolmie! Herb. Hooker)

IX. MASTIGOPHORA, Nees ab E, Gottsche, Lindenb et Nees Syn Hepat p 241.
1. *M diclados*, Brid, Web in Prodr. Spreng. Syst. Veg. vol. iv p 224 —Pacific Islands (Nightingale! Herb Hooker), Samoa (Powell!), Upolu (Græffe!)

X HERPOCLADIUM (gen nov.), Mitt. Caulis vage prolifero-ramosus, flagellis elongatis descendentibus ventralibus Folia amphigastriaque conformia, verticaliter inserta, integra aut apice bifida. Perianthium versus apicem caulis elongatum Flores masculi in caule primario, antheridia in axillis foliorum caulinarium disposita
1. *H. bidens* (sp. nov), Mitt; caulis procumbens, geniculatus, ramis remotis elongatis, flagellisque ex axilla amphigastriorum oriundis divaricatis, ramosus, folia amphigastriaque coæqualia, patentia divaricatave, ovato-oblonga, apice subobliqua, sinu brevi angustissimo oblique bidentata, lacinis acutis, e cellulis oblongis firmis crassiusculis areolata, folia involucralia imbricata; perianthium angustum, elongatum, inferne teres, apice obtuse trigonum, ore dentatum —Sandwich Islands, inter *Jungermanniam flexicaulem* aliasque species *Hepaticarum* (Hillebrand!) —To the unassisted eye this curious plant appears, when in the dry state, very much like a slender state of *Sendtnera juniperina*, but when the foliage is moistened it is seen that the leaves are as it entire, for the cleft at the apex is so narrow that it is not at first perceptible, and the amphigastria being hardly distinguishable from the leaves, give the stems the appearance of having three equal series of leaves The perianth is similar to that of *Lepidozia*, but the whole habit and appearance of the stems and foliage is different from both *Lepidozia* and *Mastigobryum*. The only other known species referable to this genus is the *Jungermannia tenacifolia*, Hook f. et Tayl Crypt. Antarct. pl. 64 f. 6, which, although closely resembling the species from the Sandwich Islands, has its leaves and stipules undivided.

XI. Mastigobryum, Nees, Lindenb et Gottsche Syn Hepat 214

1 *M pallidum* (sp nov), caulis dichotomus, arcuatus, decurvatus; folia divaricata, devexa, ovato-ligulata, apice abrupta, tridentata, basi anguste cum amphigastrio quadrato-rotundato apice suberenato coalita.—Samoa, Upolu (Powell! forma major sub n. 91, et gracilior sub n 83), Aneitum (Knight)—Caulis 2 uncias longus, cum foliis latitudine in forma majore bilinearis, in forma graciliore sesquilineares. Folia pallide viridia, subglauca Affinis *M Novæ-Hollandiæ*, foliis autem margine integerrimis.

2 *M. subacutum* (sp nov), caulis ascendens, dichotomus; folia divaricata, subdevexa, ovato-ligulata, apice oblique truncata, tridenticulata, integerrima, margine ventrali sinuata, recurva, basi cum amphigastrio orbiculato quadrato integro apice suberenato anguste coalita.—Samoa, Upolu, on trees (1000–2000 ft) (Powell! n. 87)—Caulis biuncialis latitudine, cum foliis trilineares Folia olivaceo-viridia.—*M Novæ-Zelandiæ* simile, sed foliis apice angustiore oblique truncato subacutis breviter dentatis

3 *M pusillum* (sp. nov.); caulis pusillus, horizontalis, dichotomus, folia patula, ovato-oblonga, obtusa vel oblique abrupta, tridentata, integerrima, per medium cellulis majoribus pellucidioribus vittata, amphigastria parva, quadrato-rotunda, integra, basi anguste cum foliis connexa.—Samoa (Powell!)—Caulis subuncialis, parum divisus, cum foliis ⅓ lineam latus Folia pallide viridia.—*M integro* simile, sed amphigastriis caulem latitudine haud excedentibus et foliis cellulis majoribus vittatis diversum

4 *M serrulatum* (sp nov), caulis ascendens, parce dichotome divisus, folia divaricata, late ovata, apice abrupta, uni-bi-tridentata, margine ventrali sinuata, dorsalique serrulata, amphigastria orbiculato-ovata, integerrima vel apice subdentata.—Samoa, Upolu, on trees (1000–2000 ft) (Powell! n 86)—Caulis 3 uncias altus, cum foliis latitudine lineam parum superans Folia olivaceo-fusca.—*M eroso* simile, foliis autem divaricatis, latere ventrali magis sinuatis evidentiusque serrulatis

5 *M cordistipulum*, Mont Voy de la Bonite, Crypt t 119. f. 1 (*Herpetium*)—Sandwich Islands (Gaudichaud, n 89, Hillebrand, n 11; Tolmie, Douglas, n 70), Hawaii (Beechey! Macrae!)

6 *M dentatum* (sp. nov.), caulis ascendens, dichotomus, folia devexa, ovato-ligulata, apice dentibus tribus acuminatis, margine ventrali sinuato, basi auricula rotundata denticulata, amphigastria magna, quadrato-rotundata, basi cordata, ubique dentibus spinosis ciliata.—Samoa, Manua, damp trees (2000 ft) (Powell! n 92)—Caulis triuncialis latitudine, cum foliis bilinearis Folia olivacea, fuscescentia.—*M paradoxa*, Sande, Lacoste Syn Hep Javan t 9, simile, sed foliis ad basin marginis ventralis dilatata et lobulo dentato auctis diversum.

XII. Mastigopelma (gen. nov), Mitt. Caulis superne simplex, inferne ramos stoloniformes et innovationes emittens Folia amphigastriaque integra. Fructus basilaris.—The small species upon which this genus is proposed to be established differs in habit from *Mastigobryum*, the ascending stems not being continuous indefinitely as in that genus, but the growth of new and simple stems is renewed from the base, and the fructification appears to arise from the stoloniform shoots, which form the substratum of the plants.

1 *M simplex* (sp nov), Mitt, caulis ascendens, inferne foliis abbreviatis parvis rotundatis appressis sparsim dispositis stolonibus attenuatis repentibus intertextus, superne innovationibus simplicibus, ramosus; folia planiuscula, patentia, late ovalia, margine dorsali apiceque rotundato denticulata, amphigastria parva, subquadrata, apice erosa patula, involucrum ad ramorum basin, foliis complicatis patulis apice denticulatis.—Samoa, growing on rotten wood in a tufted manner (Powell!)—Rami 3–4 lineas longi, latitudine, cum foliis ⅔-lineares, siccitate recurvi—A small brown plant, which at first sight resembles in its simple stems and the form of its foliage some of the smaller species of *Plagiochila*.

XIII. Lepidozia, Nees, Lindenb. et Gottsche Syn Hepat 200

1. *L. infuscata* (sp nov), Mitt, caulis elongatus, solidus, fuscus, demum nigricans; folia patentia, subovata, tri-quadridentata, ramea suboblonga, quadridentata, amphigastria parva, sub-semiorbiculata, indistincte quadridentata.—Samoa (Powell! n 158).—Caules 2–4 uncias altus, ramis 1½ unciam longis Folia inconspicua

2 *L. Sandwichensis*, Lindenb. Sp Hepat t 1—*L filipendula*, Tayl Lond Journ. of Bot 1846, p 368—Sandwich Islands (Tolmie! Herb Hooker)—Caulis 2 uncias altus, pallide fuscus

3. *L fistulosa* (sp. nov), caulis elongatus, fistulosus, pallidus, ramis breviusculis curvatis decurvis; folia minuta, appressa, ovato-quadrata, tri-quadridentata; amphigastria semiorbicularia, subintegra.—Samoa (Powell!).—Caulis biuncialis, ramis 3–4 lineas longis attenuatis, pallide fuscus—*L Sandwichensi* colore similis, sed gracilior, foliis brevioribus

4 *L brevidentata* (sp. nov); caulis procumbens, elongatus, pinnatus, folia explanata, parva, subquadrata, breviter quadridentata, segmentis acutis, amphigastria parva, patentia, quadridentata.—Samoa (Powell!)—Caulis cum foliis vix ⅓ lineam latus—*L capilligeræ*, Sch (*Jungermannia*) simillima, sed folia dentibus brevioribus

5. *L australis*, Lehm et Lindenb in Lehm. Pug vol. vi—*L reptans*, β *australis*, Gottsche, Lindenb et Nees Syn. Hepat 205 *L triceps*, Tayl Lond Journ of Bot. 1846, p 369.—Hawaii (Menzies!)—

Caules quadrilineares, depressi   Folia fusco-viridia, pallida, dentibus obtusiusculis.—Similar to the European *L. reptans*

XIV. PHYSIOTIUM, Nees ab E., Gottsche, Lindenb et Nees Syn Hep 234
1. *P sphagnoides*, Richard, Hook. Musc Exot. t 47 (*Jungermannia*)—Hawaii (Herb. Hooker, fide Syn Hepat. 721)
2. *P. conchæfolium*, Hook et Arn. in Beechey's Voy t 23 (*Jungermannia*)—Hawaii (Beechey!), Sandwich Islands (Hillebrand! n 8)
3 *P evolutum* (sp nov), Mitt, rami ascendentes, incurvati, folia secunda imbricata, lobo dorsali ovato apice oblique sinu parvo acuto bidentato margine superiore basin versus subdentato, lobo ventrali subæquilongo ovato evoluta, concava, basi margine incurva, folia involucralia exserta, laxe appressa; perianthia in glomeris decurvatis disposita, cylindracea, lævia, ore obtuso inflexo—Hawaii (Macrae! Herb Mus Brit)—*P. sphagnoidi P. conchæfolio*que similis, sed diversum lobulis evolutis

XV NOTOSCYPHUS (gen nov), Mitt Caulis procumbens prostratusve, ex apice fertilis Folia integra, planiuscula Amphigastria parva Perianthium nullum.
1 *N lutescens*, Lehm et Lindenb (*Jungermannia*), caulis simplex, plus minus elongatus; folia horizontalia, expansa vel sursum curvata conniventique, ovali-rotundata vel apice subangulata; amphigastria lanceolata, profunde bifida, laciniis contiguis, folia involucralia majora, sursum curvata, imbricata, apice angustiora dentata, inferne concava—*Gymnomitrium lutescens*, Gottsche; idem, Lindenb et Nees Syn Hepat p 4—Samoa (Powell, n 151)—Caulis interdum unciam longus, cum folis lineam latis Folia pallide albo-viridia, siccitate vix mutata—There appears to be no difference between these specimens and those from India and Java In this species the fruit appears to arise from the dorsal side of the apex of the stem

XVI SACCOGYNA, Dumort , Gottsche, Lindenb. et Nees Syn Hepat p 191
1 *S jugata* (sp nov), Mitt ; caulis elongatus, parum divisus, folia explanata, ovata, basi dorsali connexa, apice obtusa, integra vel uni-bi-tridenticulata, cellulis rotundis obscuris, ad folii margines prominulis interstitiis angustis intercalaribus nullis distinctis; amphigastria parva, laciniis ovatis acutis—Samoa, creeping over other *Hepaticæ* (Powell).—Caules 1-2 uncias longi, cum folis 1½ lineam lati. Folia pallide fusca.—*S australi* Novæ Zelandiæ minor, et folis antice conjugatis distincta.

XVII CALYPOGEIA, Raddi, Gottsche, Lindenb. et Nees Syn Hepat. p. 197
1. *C Trichomanis*, Spreng.—Sandwich Islands.

XVIII SYMPHOGYNA, Mont. et Nees, Gottsche, Lindenb et Nees Syn. Hepat p. 179
1 *S subsimplex*, Mitt in Fl Nov. Zeland. vol ii p 166—Sandwich Islands (Hillebrand, n 3), Samoa (Powell).—The habit and appearance of this species is that of *Steetzia*

I **Plagiochila**, Nees et Mont.; Gottsche, Lindenb. et Nees Syn Hepat. p. 22.   Caulis primarius repens, ramos ascendentes simplices dichotomos, rarius pinnatos ferens. Folia integerrima vel dentata; amphigastria nulla vel in speciebus paucissimis obvia. Perianthium compressum, læve, ore truncato vel bilabiato.

A very extensive genus, of which the species are most abundant in the intertropical regions   They are not susceptible of being divided into well-defined sections. The following are Polynesian species not yet found in Viti, viz.—1 *P fissidentoides*, Tayl Loud Journ of Bot 1816; Gottsche, Lindenb et Nees Syn Hepat. p. 636—Sandwich Islands (Menzies!)—Compared by Taylor to *P. bursata*   *P Vitiense* may be the complete state of *P. fissidentoides*, but it does not suggest any comparison with *P. bursata*, with which Taylor contrasts it   2 *P bialata* (sp nov.), Mitt., rami graciles, subsimplices, intra perianthium innovatione singula proliferi, folia remotiuscula, explanata, lata, subovata, obtusa, margine ventrali apiceque parce dentata, dorsali integerrima recurva, involucralia majora magis dentata; perianthium late obovatum, labiis subtruncatis dentatis antice posticeque anguste alatum, ala angusta brevidentata—Samoa (Powell!).—Rami 1-2 uncias alti, cum folis sesquilineam lati. Folia obscura, fusca. 3. *P pacifica* (sp. nov), Mitt , rami elongati, superne dichotome divisi, folia explanata, patentia, dimidiato-cordata, subligulata, obtusa, in ramis attenuatis conformia, apice truncato-bidentata, apice margineque ventrali spinoso-dentata, dorsali recurva, dentibus parvis remotis inconspicuis.—Sunday Island, ad arbores (Milne! n 87).—Rami 2-3 uncias alti, cum folis latitudine bilineares. 4. *P. longispica* (sp. nov.), Mitt , rami humiles vel elongati, apice dichotome divisi; folia explanata, divergentia, semicordato-oblonga, obtusa, in partibus ulterioribus oblonga, margine ubique dentibus parvis spinulosis dentata, dorsali recurva, ventrali basi in auriculam parvam tumidam revoluta, involucralia parum diversa; perianthium obovatum, ala nulla, ore truncato dentato, spicæ

3 G 2

masculæ elongatæ interdum ramosæ, foliis perigonialibus brevibus concavis integerrimis —Samoa (Powell!
n. 58) —Rami 1-4 uncias alti, latitudine cum foliis bilineares   Folia luteo-viridia vel olivacea   Spicæ
masculæ ½-1½ unciam longæ, curvatæ   5   *P auriculata* (sp nov), Mitt., rami elongati, simplices vel fasciculatim dichotomi , folia explanata, a basi latiora, semicordata, angustata, ligulata, obtusa, margine ubique
dentibus elongatis angustis ciliata, angulo ventrali in auriculam inflatam revoluto, involucralia magis ciliata
—Samoa (Powell! n 6) —Rami 1-2-unciales, latitudine cum foliis bilineares   Folia mollia, olivaceo-viridia
6. *P. combinata* (sp nov), Mitt., caulis innovatione singula infra perianthium orta iterum iterumque
continuatus , folia opposita, remotiuscula, patula, oblongo-elliptica, apice bidentata, margine dorsali præcipue
apicem versus paucidentata, basi antice posticeque anguste combinata, folia involucralia margine dorsali
ventraliquo magis dentata, perianthio late obovato, ala parva antica dentata, labiis grosse dentatis —Sandwich Islands (Hillebrand! n 29) —Caulis subuncialis, gracilis   Folia lineam longa, fulvo-viridia —In the
form of its leaves, this curious species resembles *P ærea*, Tayl., and is remote from any other with conju-
gate leaves   7 *P. oblongiflora*, rami graciles, parce dichotome divisi, folia remota, late ovata, obtusa,
margine ventrali apiceque breviter dentata, dorsali integerrima, involucralia margine conformia; perianthium elongatum, oblongum, apice truncatum dentatum, ala nulla, spicæ masculæ sæpe interruptæ foliis perigonialibus
obtusis vel acutis —Samoa (Powell! n 51) —Rami 1-2-unciales, cum foliis sesquilinea lati   Folia firma,
obscure fusca 8 *P. Owathensis*, Nees ab E et Lindenb , Lindenb Sp Hepat. fasc. 1 t 5 —Hawaii
(Menzies!).

1. **P. arbuscula,** Brid. (*Jungermannia*), Lindenb Sp Hepat. f. 1. t. 4; rami elongati, superne
dichotomi, flabelliforme divisi, folia explanata, patentia, dimidiata, ovata, apice oblique truncata,
dentibus duobus validioribus, margine ventrali paucidentata, dorsali recurvo integerrimo, involucralia magis dentata; perianthium ovato-oblongum, ore parvo, labiis rotundatis denticulatis; perigonia
in ramis elongatis interrupta, foliis apice subtridentatis —Also in Viti (Seemann! inter n. 862;
Milne!), Samoa (Powell!), Upolu (Græffe!).

Rami in speciminibus Vitiensibus triunciales, latitudine cum foliis 1-1½-lineares   Folia nigro-fusca

2. **P. Vitiensis,** Mitt. Bonplandia, 1861, p 367; rami superne dichotomi; folia explanata,
patentia, oblongo-ligulata, apice obtusa, in superiora oblique truncata, margine dorsali recurva,
integerrima, ventrali parum curvata, apicem versus apiceque dentata, involucralia latiora, apice margineque ventrali spinoso-ciliata , perianthium obovatum, ala nulla, ore labiis subtruncatis dentato-
ciliatis —*P. patentissima*, ex parte, Gottsche, Lindenb. et Nees Syn. Hep. 36.—Viti (Seemann!
n 862).   Also in Hawaii (Menzies! in Herb Hooker).

Rami biunciales, cum foliis latitudine vix bilineares.   Folia viridia.

3. **P. Seemanni,** Mitt. 'Bonplandia,' 1861, p 367; rami elongati, simplices; folia explanata,
divaricata, semicordato-ovata, obtusa, in partibus superioribus ramorum attenuatis magis rotundata,
margine toto ambitu breviter spinoso dentata, ventrali basi reflexa, dorsali recurva, basi subsinuata,
e cellulis parvis rotundis interstitiis grossis areolata.—Viti (Seemann ! n. 864).

Rami 2-5 uncias alti, latitudine cum foliis 4-lineares   Folia olivaceo-viridia —*P. superbæ*, Nees ab E ,
insulæ Mauritii simillima, sed foliis obtusis margine ubique dentatis

4. **P. geminifolia,** (sp. nov.) Mitt. ; rami erecti, geniculati, proliferi, ramulis flagelliformi-
attenuatis descendentibus , folia verticalia opposita, basi connexa, patentia, late obovata, apice
rotundata, dentibus latis brevibus serrata, margine dorsali ventralique integerrima, involucralia
dentibus majoribus lanceolatis denticulata ; perianthium obovatum, compressum, labiis dentibus
pluribus elongatis, ciliatum ; folia perigonialia imbricata, saccata, apice tridentata —Viti (Seemann!).
Also in Samoa (Powell! n. 50).

Caules fertiles innovationibus uncialibus iterum iterumque proliferi, interdum 3-4 uncias alti, masculi
unciales, apice attenuati arcuati descendentesque.
So similar is this to *P opposita*, Nees, found in Java and Ceylon, that until the perianths were
detected it was supposed to be a state of that species, but it differs in the following particulars.—The
cauline leaves are not rotund, but obovate or subcuneate , those embracing the perianth are strongly

toothed with teeth which are also themselves dentate, and the perianth is broadly obovate; the lips rounded, and with many long teeth. Fragments of this species were mentioned in 'Bonplandia' as *P. opposita* and *P. Brauniana.*

II. **Jungermannia,** Linn. Caulis procumbens, subsimplex. Folia explanata vel sursum secunda, integra vel dentata, amphigastria parva vel nulla. Perianthium tubulosum, inferne læve, superne plicatum, ore contractum, dentatum.

The three following species have not yet been discovered in Viti, viz. —1 *J contracta*, Nees ab E ; Gottsch Lindenb et Nees Syn Hep 79 —Samoa (Powell!). 2. *J piligera*, Nees ab E ; Gottsch Lindenb. et Nees Syn Hep t 81 —Sandwich Islands, with *J. contracta* (Hillebrand! Meyen!), Samoa (Powell!) 3 *J Liebeckii*, Mont Ann des Sc Nat 1843, p 247.—Sandwich Islands (Gaudichaud!).

1. **J. flexicaulis,** Nees ab E.; Gottsche, Lindenb. et Nees Syn. Hepat. p. 87; caulis procumbens, flexuosus, e ventre proliferus; folia densa, sursum secunda complicataque, cordato-orbiculata concava, apice obtusa vel angulata, margine ventrali inflexo recto, dorsali flexuoso integerrima, cellulis parvis areolata, involucralia integra vel obtuse bi-tridentata; perianthium apice denticulatum —Viti (Seemann!), Sandwich Islands (Tolmie, Herb. Hooker; Hillebrand! n. 9).

Originally described from Java, where it is said to be frequent. It is found as far south as New Zealand.

III. **Chiloscyphus,** Corda; Gottsche, Lindenb et Nees Syn. Hepat. 171. Caulis procumbens. Folia explanata vel sursum secunda; amphigastria bi-quadri-pluridentata. Perianthium in ramulo brevi laterale, campanulatum, ore subtruncatum.

The species comprised in this genus are in habit and general appearance intimately related to *Lophocolea*, and, as in that genus, they are divisible into a green and a brown group, but in a less well-defined manner

The following are non-Vitian Polynesian species:—1 *C decurrens* (sp. nov), Mitt , caulis procumbens, elongatus ; folia sursum secunda, opposita, ovata, obtusa, integerrima, margine dorso coalita, ventre cum amphigastrio orbiculari dentato confluentia, cellulis rotundis spatiis intercalaribus distinctis areolata, folia involucralia parva, concava, dentata, perianthium tubulosum, superne plicatum, ore dentato ciliatum —Sandwich Islands (Nightingale), Samoa (Powell! n. 76). Also in Java and Penang 2 *C. coalitus*, Hook —Aneitum (Milne! n. 874), Isle of Pines (Strange!).

1. **C. confluens,** (sp. nov.) Mitt.; caulis procumbens; folia sursum secunda, opposita, subtriangularia, apice sinu parvo rotundato biciliato-dentata vel subintegra, margine dorsali subrecta, undulata, basi connexa, ventrali rotundata, incurva, basi cum amphigastrio magno reniformi-rotundato, apice quadridentata, dentibus interioribus longioribus confluente.—Foliis biciliatis, Viti (Seemann !); foliis apice uni- vel sub-bidentatis, Samoa (Powell !).

Statura habituque *C decurrenti* simillima, sed foliis diversiformibus

2. **C. Endlicherianus,** Nees ab E., Gottsche, Lindenb. et Nees Syn. Hepat. 184; caulis prostratus, elongatus ; folia explanata, oblonga, obtusa, apice integerrima vel denticulis brevibus munita ; amphigastria parva, quadrispinosa, uno latere angustissime in folio proximo decurrente; perianthium compressum, apice dentatum.—Viti (Seemann !), Norfolk Island (Herb. Hooker), Solomon Islands (Milne!), Samoa (Powell! n. 157).

This species, which is found also in Australia and New Zealand, seems to differ from *C argutus*, so widely distributed in south-eastern Asia, in its more oblong leaves, in other respects the resemblance is very close. The Norfolk Island specimens have a terebinthine odour, which is scarcely perceptible in those from Samoa

IV. **Radula,** Nees ab E.; Gottsche, Lindenb. et Nees Syn Hepat. 253. Caulis procumbens, pinnatus, rarius dichotomus Folia lobo ventrali minore appresso, basi cauli adhærente, medio sæpe tumidulo radicellas emittente Amphigastria nulla. Perianthium campanulatum, elongatum, complanatum, læve, rarius plicatum, ore truncatum, bilabiatum.

The following are non-Vitian species —1 *R Javanica*, Gottsche, idem Lindenb. et Nees Syn Hepat. p 257 —*R cordiloba*, Tayl Lond Journ of Bot 1846, p 375 —Hawaii (Menzies), Pacific Islands (Nightingale; Herb Hooker), Samoa (Powell, n. 160) 2. *R. decurrens* (sp. nov.), Mitt., caulis ramis breviusculis patentibus, plumæformi-pinnatus, folia explanata, dorso convexa, divergentia, oblongo-ovalia, obtusa, margine ubique incurva, lobulo subquadrato caulem tegente, basi subcordato decurrente, margine exteriore revoluto, carina plicaturæ in caulem longe descendente —Samoa (Powell!) —Caulis 3-4 uncias longus, ramis semiuncialibus, cum folis lineam lati Folia olivacea, subfusca —*R Javanicæ* similis, folis autem angustioribus, lobulo majore, angulo insertionis exteriore et carina in caulem decurrente —This robust species, at first sight, resembles some of the species of *Madotheca*. 3 *R cordata* (sp. nov.), Mitt, caulis rigidus, procumbens, pinnatus, folia imbricata, late ovata, obtusa, divergentia, basi dorsali semicordata, lobulo magno subrotundo, apice obtuse angulato, basi supra caulem late protracto rotundato semicordato auriculato, carina in caulem descendente, apice sinuata —Sandwich Islands (Hillebrand!) —Rami biunciales, cum folis lineam lati Folia flavo-fusca —Habit and size of *R. decurrens*, and, like it, more resembling *Madotheca Stangeri* in general appearance than any of the other species of *Radula* 4 *R reflexa*, Nees et Mont ; Mont. in Voy de la Bonite Bot Crypt. t 117 f 3 —Sandwich Islands (Gaudichaud!) 5 *R retroflexa*, Tayl. Lond. Journ of Bot 1846, p. 378 —Pacific Islands (Nightingale, Herb Hooker). 6 *R pinnulata* (sp nov), Mitt, caulis gracilis, procumbens, pinnatus ; folia explanata, ovato-orbiculata, lobulo subquadrato angulo apicali semitorto, basali cordato, caulem tegente —Isle of Pines (Strange) —Caulis 1-1½ unciam longus, ramis sesquilinearibus, cum folis latitudine semilineam metiens. Folia olivaceo viridia —*R bucciniferæ*, Tayl., subsimilis, sed caule magis plumæformi pinnato. 7. *R acuta* (sp nov.), Mitt., caulis gracilis, pinnatim divisus, folia orbiculato-ovata, acuta apiculitave, subintegerrima vel præcipue margine dorsali denticulata, lobulo parvo acuto —Isle of Pines (Strange), Pacific Islands, on a species of *Trichomanes* (ex Herb Ward) —Caulis circiter semiunciam longus, cum folis semilineam latus Folia viridia, fuscescentia —*R. ancipiti*, Sande Lacoste, Syn. Hepat. Javan t 10, simillima, sed folis in caule primario sæpe integerrimis, lobulo diversiformi acuto.

1. R. spicata, Mitt. 'Bonplandia,' 1862, p. 19; caulis prostratus, vage divisus ; folia subreniformia, apice devexa, incurva, lobulo oblongo appresso usque ad medium marginis ventralis producto, apice obtuse angulato, perianthio oblongo compresso lævi; amentula mascula parva, brevia.—Viti (Seemann ! n. 837).

Caulis unciam longus, cum folis semilineam latus Folia olivaceo-fusca —*R. formosæ* et *R scariosæ* similis, sed foliis angustioribus et lobulo diversiformi.

2. R. amentulosa, Mitt. 'Bonplandia,' 1861, p. 367; caulis prostratus, vage ramosus ; folia devexa, subreniformia, apice rotundata, lobulo satis magno obovato apice rotundato ad medium folii margine ventrali producto appresso; perianthium campanulatum, læve, spicis masculis parvis amentiformibus.—Viti (Seemann ! inter n. 837).

Caulis semiuncialis, latitudine cum folis ¼-linearis Folia olivaceo-viridia —*R formosæ* similis sed minor, et folia angustiora, lobulo apice rotundato, sensim versus basin angustato; amentula mascula nunc brevia triphylla, nunc elongata exserta.

3 R. scariosa, Mitt. 'Bonplandia,' 1861, p. 367, caulis prostratus, vage ramosus ; folia suborbiculata, convexa, apice incurva, lobulo subovali appresso ad medium usque marginis ventralis producto, apice rotundato scarioso-hyalino marginato, amentulis masculis brevibus, perianthio oblongo compresso lævi.—Viti (Seemann ! inter n. 837).

Caulis semiunciam longus, cum folis semilineam latus Folia fusca —*R. formosa* paululo minor, folis magis orbiculatis convexisque.

V. Madotheca, Dumort.; Gottsche, Lindenb. et Nees Syn Hepat. p. 262. Caulis procumbens, pinnatus. Folia lobo ventrali parvo appresso. Amphigastria integra. Perianthium campanulatum, compressum, ore integro bilabiato dentatove.

The following is a non-Vitian species.—*M. viridissima* (sp nov), Mitt ; caulis elongatus, ramis divaricatis pinnatus; folia explanata, ovata, obtusissima, lobulo parvo anguste oblongo integerrimo, amphigastria ovato-oblonga, obtusa, integerrima.—Samoa (Powell! n 161)—Caulis 3-4 uncias longus, ramis semiuncialibus latitudine, cum foliis lineam metiens. Folia intense viridia.—A *M. Stangeri* foliis magis ovatis, amphigastrii forma magis ovata angustis, et lobulo angustiore diversa.

1. **M. Stangeri,** Lindenb. et Gottsche, iidem et Nees Syn. Hepat. p 280 ; caulis elongatus, ramis divergentibus pinnatus; folia dorso convexa, orbiculato-oblonga, lobulo late ovali, amphigastrioque oblongo-rotundo, margine recurvo integerrimo; folia involucralia denticulata, perianthio labiis denticulatis.—Viti (Seemann !), Tahiti (Collie in Herb. Mus. Brit.).

Specimens all without fruit, but to all appearance not different from the states of this species so abundant in New Zealand

VI. Bryopteris, Lindenb.; Gottsche, Lindenb. et Nees Syn. Hepat. 281. Caulis primarius repens, radicans, ramos elongatos liberos ramosos ascendentes dependentesve prodens. Folia lobulo parvo involuto; amphigastria integra. Fructus e latere ad caulis apicem spectante ramulorum lateralium oriundus. Perianthium plicatum.

The following species is non-Vitian:—*B. vittata* (sp. nov.), Mitt., rami graciles, elongati, ramulis breviusculis remotis, pinnatim ramosi; folia patenti-divergentia, ovata, acuta, margine apicem versus dentata, basi ventrali subdecurrentia, lobulo minuto suboblongo unidentato inflexo appendiculo parvo alaeformi carinato, cellulis in folii medio majoribus ovalibus vittam fuscidulam formantibus reliquis rotundis; amphigastria patentia, basi cordato-auriculata, subovata, apice sinu obtuso bidentata, lateribus reflexis conniventibus remote breviterque denticulatis.—Samoa (Graeffe!), Tutuila (Powell!).—Rami 1-6 uncias longi, ramulis uncialibus patentibus, cum foliis lineam lati. Folia fusco-olivacea, sicca arcte inflexa.—The specimens, which are not in a fertile state, are more slender with more remote branchlets than is usual in *B Sinclairii* or *B striata*, but in other respects closely resemble those species, from both of which, however, they are immediately distinguished by the leaves.

* *Eubryopteris* —Perianthium dorso planum, ventre unicarinatum.

1. **B. Sinclairii,** Mitt. 'Bonplandia,' 1862, p. 19; rami elongati, pinnati; folia patentia, ovato-oblonga, obtusa, apice denticulis paucis brevibus, margine ventrali incurva, lobulo parvo involuto in foliis ramulinis unidentato, cellulis parvis oblongis subobscuris; amphigastria oblongo-ovalia, apice obtusa, paucidentata, lateribus recurvis, folia involucralia lobulique elongate late lanceolati, acuti, breviter dentati; amphigastrium ad medium usque in laciniis duabus lanceolatis fissum; perianthium dorso planum, ventre unicarinatum, angulis denticulatis.—Viti (Sinclair! Seemann! inter n. 843), Samoa (Powell! n. 152).

Rami 4-12-unciales, ramulis subuncialibus simplicibus ramulosisve. Folia olivacea, firma, lineam longa, sicca inflexa.
This species differs from *Bryopteris filicina*, Swartz, so widely distributed in South America, in its more elongated fronds, which are more produced at their apices, as if they would be indefinitely continuous

** *Ptychanthus*, Nees ab E.; Gottsche, Lindenb. et Nees Syn Hepat p 289 —Perianthium subcompressum, 8-10-plicatum

2. **B. striata,** Lehm. et Lindenb.; rami elongati, pinnati; folia divergentia, oblongo-ovalia, obtusiuscula subacutave, apice denticulata, lobulo minuto ovali involuto, amphigastria rotundata, apice retusa, denticulata, folia involucralia minora, acuta; perianthium obovatum, compressum, decemplicatum.—Viti (Milne).

Rami 3-4 uncias longi, ramis uncialibus, cum foliis lineam lati. Folia olivaceo-fuscescentia.
These specimens do not appear to differ from those from India

VII. Phragmicoma, Dumort.; Gottsche, Lindenb et Nees Syn. Hepat. p. 292. Caules procumbentes ascendentesve, dichotome rarius subpinnatim ramosi. Folia lobulo inflexo uni-bi-tridentato. Amphigastria integra, rarissime bifida. Fructus terminalis demum ob innovationes in dichotomia. Perianthium læve vel plicatum.

The following are non-Vitian species, viz —1 *P. spathulistipa*, Nees ab E Hep. Javan. p 38 (*Jungermannia*) —*Thysananthus spathulistipus*, Lindenb ; Gottsche, Lindenb et Nees Syn Hepat. p 287 —Samoa (Powell, n. 167), Upolu (Græffe). 2 *P. ligulata*, Lehm et Lindenb in Lehm Pugil vi p 39 (*Jungermannia*) —*P. ligulata*, Gottsche, Lindenb et Nees Syn Hepat p 301.—Tahiti (Beechey), Samoa (Powell) 3. *P. cuneistipula* (sp nov), Mitt ; rami breves, parce furcatim divisi, folia patentia, orbiculato-ovata, subacuta, margine ventrali incurva, lobulo parvo quadrato unidentato, amphigastria obovata, subcuneata, apice subsinuata ; folia involucralia conformia, amphigastrium retusum ; perianthium triplicatum —Isle of Pines (Milne, Strange), Pacific Islands (Beechey) —Rami 4 lineas longi, cum foliis ⅔ lineam lati Folia fuscoolivacea 4. *P. tumida*, Nees et Mont , Gottsche, Lindenb et Nees Syn. Hep p 300 (*Phragmicoma*) —Samoa (Powell) 5 *P. olivacea*, Tayl Lond Journ Bot 1844, p 568 —Samoa (Powell), Raiatea (Sibbald). 6. *P. securifolia*, Endl Prodr Fl Ins Norfolk; Gottsche, Lindenb et Nees Syn. Hepat. p 300 —Norfolk Island (Endlicher). 7 *P aulacophora*, Mont Ann des Sc. Nat Bot tom xix p 259, Voy. au Pôle Sud, t. 19 f 1 ; rami procumbentes, inordinate dichotomi, folia imbricata, sensim perianthium versus majora, suborbiculata, margine ventrali medio sinuata, lobulo oblongo, apice bidentato; amphigastria orbiculata , folia involucralia concava, apice emarginata, lobis subæqualibus inferiore acuto, amphigastrium magnum, integerrimum, perianthium oblongum, breve, immersum, demum capsula matura exserta emergens, pluries plicatum —Samoa (Powell), Manga Reva, ad radices arborum (Hombron). 8. *P immersa* (sp nov), Mitt , caulis brevis, ramosus, folia divergentia, oblongo-orbiculata, margine ventrali lobulo rotundato involuto ; amphigastria orbiculata , folia involucralia subrotunda, majora, margine dorsali apiceque dentata, lobulo parvo dentiformi , amphigastrium magnum, integerrimum, orbiculatum , perianthium inclusum, obovatum, dorso planum, ventre bicarinatum, angulis denticulis spinulosis curvulis in serie duplici dispositis ciliatis —Samoa (Powell !) —Caulis 3-4 lineas longus, cum foliis ⅔ lineam latus Folia castaneo-fusca 9 *P. tecta* (sp nov), Mitt ; caulis procumbens, ramosus ; folia divergentia, ovali-rotunda, lobulo ovato inflexo , amphigastria parva, orbiculata ; folia involucralia magna, lobulo oblongo angulo recto terminato, perianthium rotundato-obovatum, margine late alatum, ala apice dentata, dorso planum, ventre carinis duabus superne dentatis —Raoul Island, Kermandec Islands (M'Gillivray) —Caulis semiunciam longus, cum foliis semilineam latus Folia olivacea, involucralia perianthium tegentia 10 *P subnuda* (sp nov), caulis elongatus, prostratus, ramis remotis, subpinnatus; folia divergentia, ovato-rotunda, obtusa, integerrima, lobulo ovato involuto , amphigastria orbiculata , folia involucralia ovalia, subdentata, lobulo oblongo plano, apice rectangulo ; perianthium obovatum, emergens, dorso planum, læve vel plica parva, ventre bicarinatum plicis, ala angusta inconspicua remote breviterque dentata —Sandwich Islands (Hillebrand) —Caulis sesquiunciam longus, cum foliis lineam latus Folia nigro-fusca 11. *P. contractilis* (sp nov), Mitt., caulis repens, pinnatus, ramis fertilibus ascendentibus, folia divaricata, ovali-oblonga, obtusa, margine dorsali apiceque denticulata, ventrali integerrima, lobulo parvo oblongo inflexo unidentato ; amphigastria rotundo-obcordata, apice denticulata , folia involucralia ovata, acuta, margine dorsali dentata, lobulo angusto inconspicuo , amphigastrium rotundo-ovale, apice denticulatum, dentibus duobus mediis majoribus , perianthium obovatum, compressum, dorso planum, ventre apicem versus plica parva humile carinatum, margine superne denticulatum —Samoa, ad arborum corticem (Powell !) —Caules repentes, unciam longi, ramis ascendentibus 2-3-linearis, cum foliis lineam lati Folia olivacea, siccitate contracta, e cellulis subovalibus mollibus areolata

1. **P. plana**, Van der Sande Lacoste, Hep Javan. t 10 (*Thysananthus*) , rami graciles, elongati, rigiduli, dichotomi vel subpinnati , folia parva, patentia, ovali-oblonga, apice obtusa, acuta apiculatave, integerrima, margine ventrali curvata, interdum flexuosa, lobulo parvo oblongo, apice apiculo hamato ad folii marginem curvato, cellulis in folii medio majoribus ovalibus, vittam formantibus reliquis rotundatis; amphigastria rotundato-obovata, apice crenata subintegerrimave, basi medio impressa, folia involucralia erecta, elongata, apice denticulata; amphigastrium oblongum, apice sinu rectangulo bidentatum, subdenticulatum, perianthium oblongum, angulis superne denticulatis —Viti (Seemann !), Samoa (Powell), Sunday Island (Milne).

Rami 2 uncias longi, cum foliis vix semilineam lati Folia pallide olivaceo-viridia, rigidula, sicca incurva, involucralia ad perianthii apicem attingentia.—Specimens all rather more elongated than in Javan examples

2. **P. bilabiata** (sp. nov.), Mitt.; caulis breviusculus, dichotome divisus; folia patenti-diver-

gentia, rotundato-ovata, apice obtusa, margine ventrali rectiusculo, lobulo suboblongo, apice unidentato, inde sensim in folium apicem versus angustato; amphigastria orbiculata; folia involucralia minora, oblonga, perianthium obovatum, inferne teretiusculum, apice compressum, dorso depresse planum, ventre convexum bilabiatum.—Viti (Seemann!).

Caulis 4–6 lineas longus, cum foliis lineam paulo angustior. Folia flavo-viridia

3. **P. calcarata,** (sp. nov.) Mitt.; rami procumbentes, ramulis brevibus irregularibus ramosi; folia dense imbricata, patentia, rotundato-oblonga, obtusa, margine ventrali inflexa, lobulo oblongo, apice dente calcariformi terminato; amphigastria transverse latiora, subreniformia, apice recta; perianthium oblongum, obtusum, rostratum, triplicatum.—Viti, Ovalau (Seemann!).

Rami 1–1½ uncias longi, cum foliis lineam lati. Folia olivaceo-fusca.—*L. tumidæ* habitu et statura simillima, nec colore diversa, sed folis lobulo dente unico calcareformi et perianthio ventre unicarinato diversa.

4. **P. eulopha,** Tayl. Lond. Journ. of Bot. 1846, p. 391; caulis elongatus, parce ramosus; folia divaricata, oblonga, apice rotundata, incurva, margine ventrali medio sinuata, lobulo oblongo unidentato, amphigastria transversim latiora, subreniformia, margine recurva; folia involucralia majora, acutiuscula, lobulis amphigastrioque orbiculato denticulis ciliata, perianthium obovatum, immersum, dorso planum, ventre biplicatum, carinis omnibus spinoso-denticulatis.—Viti (Seemann), Pacific Islands (Nightingale).

Caulis 1–1½-uncialis, cum foliis semilineam latus. Folia fusca.

5. **P. renistipula,** (sp. nov.) Mitt.; caulis elongatus, flaccidus, ramosus; folia divergentia, ovato-rotunda, apice rotundata, denticulata, margine dorsali inflexo, ventrali lobulo parvo saccato ovato, amphigastria rotundo-reniformia; folia involucralia apice evidentius dentata, lobulo parvo acuto, amphigastrium magnum, ovali-rotundum, perianthium obovatum, compressum, dorso uni- ventre bicarinatum, plicis denticulis spinosis ciliatis.—Viti (Seemann!).

Caulis sub-biuncialis, vix cum foliis semilineam latus. Folia nigro-fusca.

VIII. **Lejeunia,** Gottsche et Lindenb., iidem et Nees Syn. Hepat. p. 308. Caules procumbentes, ascendentes vel prostrati, dichotomi vel pinnatim ramosi. Folia lobulo inflexo interdum obsoleto. Amphigastria bifida, rarius integra, in paucis speciebus duplicata vel nulla. Fructus in ramulo brevissimo lateralis. Perianthium læve aut plicatum

§ 1 *Phragmicomoideæ*, Gottsche, Lindenb. et Nees Syn. Hepat. p. 310.

The following are non-Vitian Polynesian species belonging to this section, viz.—1 *L. cryptocarpa* (sp. nov.), rami breves, parce divisi; folia patenti-divergentia, ovato-oblonga, obtusa, margine ventrali subrecta, lobulo parvo rotundo-quadrato, apice rotundato; amphigastria orbicularia, foliis triplo minora; perianthium foliis rameis obtectum, obovatum, dorso planum, ventre convexum, margine superne dentibus spinulosis ciliatum.—Hawaii, supra *Leptogium azureum* repens (Menzies!), Samoa, ad *Chætomitrium frondosum* adhærens (Powell), Isle of Pines (Strange).—Rami unciam longi, cum foliis lineam lati. Folia tenera, olivaceo-fusca.—Species *L. transversali* similis, sed minor. Perianthium absque foliis involucralibus propriis in axilla ramuli brevissimi lateralis sessile. 2. *L. squamata,* Nees ab E.; Gottsche, Lindenb. et Nees Syn. Hepat. p. 322.—Hawaii, ad *Radulam pallentem* (*R. Javanica?*).—A pale green, much-branched species, of which the typical form of the Syn. Hepat. is stated to grow in India and in Hawaii.

1. **L. procumbens,** (sp. nov.) Mitt.; caulis procumbens, parum ramosus; folia dense imbricata, divergentia, ovali-rotundata, apice incurva, margine ventrali recto, basi lobulo parvo rotundato involuto; amphigastria magna, transversim latiora, subreniformia.—Viti (Seemann).

Caulis subuncialis, cum foliis lineam latus. Folia pallide albo-viridia, cellulis parvis obscuriusculis.

[PUBLISHED JUNE 1, 1871.] 3 H

§ 2. *Omphalanthus*—Omphalanthus, Lindenb et Nees; iidem et Gottsche Syn. Hepat p 303

To this section belongs,—3 *L pedunculata* (sp. nov.), Mitt caulis elongatus, flaccidus, ramulis paucis brevissimis inconspicuis, folia divergentia, oblongo-ovalia, obtusa, apice inflexa, lobulo parvo involuto, apice dentato, amphigastria magna, orbiculata, basi cordata; folia involucralia conformia; amphigastrium apice sinu parvo excisum; perianthium pyriforme, obtusum, quinqueplicatum, inferne sensim in pedunculum teretem attenuatum—Samoa (Powell)—Caulis 2-4 uncias longus, ramulis 1-6-linearibus, cum foliis ¼ lineam latus   Folia castanea, fusca, submigra.—*L filiformi* statura similis, periantho autem longe diversa.

§ 3. *Typicæ*, Gottsche, Lindenb et Nees Syn Hepat p 325

The following non-Vitian species belong to this section —1 *L polyploca*, Tayl Lond Journ. Bot. 1846, p 396—Pacific Islands (Herb Hooker), Tahiti (Sibbald), Samoa (Powell)   5 *L anisophylla*, Mont Ann des Sc. Nat 1843, p 263, Gottsche, Lindenb et Nees Syn Hepat 377 —Sandwich Islands (Gaudichaud)

2. L. Hawaiiensis, Gottsche; idem Lindenb et Nees Syn Hepat. p 351; caulis elongatus, ramosus, folia divaricata, subdecurva, ovalia, acuta, interdum obtusa, apice inflexa, lobulo parvo ovato involuto; amphigastria cordata, sinu aperto ad medium fissa; folia involucralia parva, acuta, lobulo lanceolato; amphigastrium ovatum, laciniis utrinque extus unidentatis; perianthium clavatum, teres, apice obtusum, subinflatum.—*L microloba*, Tayl. Lond. Journ. of Bot 1846, p. 399.—Viti (Seemann !), Hawaii (Menzies), South Sea Islands (Nightingale), Samoa (Powell).

Caulis 1–2 uncias longus, cum foliis vix semilineam latus   Folia pallide fusca

3. L. uvifera, Mont Cent. vol vi. n 4. t. 6 f. 1, Syll p. 77; caulis gracilis, elongatus, parum ramosus; folia divergentia, ovalia, obtusa, apice incurva, integerrima, dorso convexa, lobulo ovato brevi saccato in caulem descendente, apice unidentato; amphigastria contigua, suborbiculata, ad medium usque bifida, laciniis acutis, folia involucralia minora, subovata, perianthium clavatum, inferne teres, apice obtusum, acute quinqueplicatum, mucrone demum in laciniis angustis fisso terminatum —*L. gracilipes*, Tayl.—Viti (Seemann), Samoa (Powell), Aneitum (ex Herb. Knight), Pacific Islands (Herb. Hooker)

Caulis subuncialis, cum foliis vix semilineam latus   Folia pallidissime luteo-fusca, lobulo satis magno tumido vel interdum fere obsoleto

4. L. crassiretis, (sp nov.) Mitt.; caulis gracilis, elongatus, folia divergentia, ovali-rotunda, obtusa, lobulo parvo ovato involuto, cellulis grossiusculis interstitiis crassis areolata, amphigastria parva, rotunda, sinu subrectangulo ad medium fissa; folia involucralia obovata, lobulo lanceolato; perianthium obovatum, obtusum, compressum, dorso uni- ventre bicarinatum.—Viti (Seemann !).

Caulis subuncialis, cum foliis semilineam latus   Folia pallide fusco-olivacea

§ 4 *Ceratanthæ*, Gottsche, Lindenb. et Nees Syn. Hepat p 395

To this section belongs the following non-Vitian species —6 *L. oceanica* (sp nov), Mitt, caulis procumbens, inordinatim subpinnatim ramosus; folia divaricata, ovato-rotunda, apice incurva, integerrima, lobulo parvo involuto, amphigastria magna, rotunda, basi cordata, apice sinu angusto breviter bidentata, lateribus incurvis, folia involucralia amphigastriumque apice dentata; perianthium obconicum, quinquecornutum —Samoa, on *Garovaglia Powellii* (Powell !), Raiatea (Collie !) —Caulis 2-uncialis debilis latitudine, cum foliis vix semilineam metiens.   Folia castanea

§ 5 *Acrogoniæ*, Mitt Linn Trans 1860, p 58 —Perianthium pentagonum, turbinatum, angulis subcornutis

The following non-Vitian species belong to this section —7. *L radiata* (sp nov), Mitt., caulis prostratus, ramosus, folia patentia, alterna, oblonga, obtusa, oblique acutave subdenticulata, lobulo parvo ovato inflexo, cellulis majoribus circiter tribus æquidistantibus sæpe vix conspicuis, amphigastria parva, ad basin usque fissa, laciniis angustis, folia involucralia parva, lobulo obsoleto, amphigastrium oblongum, apice

breviter bifidum ; perianthium obovatum, apice truncatum, angulis quinis acutis —Samoa, ad folia plantarum et in frondibus *Hymenophylloruni* ramis stellatis repens (Powell!) —Caulis 3-4 lineas longus, cum
foliis ½-⅓ lineam latus. Folio nigro-fusca —Similis est *L trematodi* 8 *L pentadactyla*, Mont Cent.
vol. vi n 3 ; Syll p 75 —Tahiti, in foliis *Crossostylis biflora* (Lepine).

5. **L. tripuncta,** (sp nov.) Mitt. ; caulis repens, ramosus ; folia patentia, alterna, sublanceolato-
ovata, margine dorsali ventralique dentibus spinosis divaricatis 2-3 armata, cellulis in folii medio
tribus majoribus pellucidis æquidistantibus in lineam dispositis, lobulo magno saccato, dimidium
folii occupante lævi ; amphigastria ad basin usque in lacinias angustas divergentibus furcata.—Viti,
in foliis *Spiridentis* (Seemann!).

Exilissima species, ramis cum foliis vix ¼ lineam latis.

§ G *Eulejeunia* —Perianthium 2-5-plicatum

The following Polynesian species belong to this section :—9 *L Samoana* (sp. nov), Mitt. ; caulis in
cæspitem depressum intricatus ; folia divergentia, rotundo-ovata, obtusa, lobulo ovato involuto, amphigastria
parva, rotunda, sinu parvo bidentata ; folia involucralia conformia, amphigastrium ovale, breviter obtuseque
bidentatum , perianthium obov ato-oblongum, obtusum, deplanatum, dorso subconcavum, ventro convexum.
—Samoa, ad corticem (Powell !) —Caulis cum foliis ¾ lineam latus. Folia fusca 10 *L effusa* (sp nov),
Mitt ; caulis repens, parum ramosus, folia divergentia, oblique ovata, obtusa, integerrima, lobulo ovato
involuto apice unidentato, amphigastria nulla ; involucralia apice latiora, rotundata, lobulo oblongo obtuso,
perianthium obcordatum, compressum, dorso planum, ventre medio convexum.—Samoa, ad frondes *Trichomanis* applane repens (Powell) —Caulis 2-6 lineas longus, cum foliis ¼ lineam latus Folia albo-viridia —
Species pusilla, foliis integerrimis, cellulis exterioribus rotundatis, interioribus autem duplo triplove majoribus oblongis 11. *L cancellata*, Nees et Mont., Gottsche, Lindenb et Nees Syn Hepat. p 385 —Sandwich Islands (Gaudichaud) —Planta exigua, aliquot linearum longitudine, fuscula, rigidula 12. *L pacifica*,
Mont Ann des Sc Nat. 1843 ; Gottsche, Lindenb et Nees Syn Hepat 378 —Sandwich Islands (Gaudichaud) 13. *L vesicata* (sp nov), Mitt , caulis arcte appressus, repens, ramosus ; folia rotunda, obtusissima,
lobulo ovato subsaccato , amphigastria orbiculata, ad ½ usque bifida ; folia involucralia subacuta, lobulis
acutis; amphigastrium oblongum, perianthium oblongo-obovatum, obtusum, quinque-plicatum, carinis
plicarum cellulis vesiculosis tumidulis asperis —Pacific Islands (Beechey!), Isle of Pines, Main Peak
(Milne!), Samoa (Powell!) —Caulis in maculas latas depressas dispositis, latitudine cum foliis ¼ lineam
metientes. Folia pallidæ olivaceo-viridia, cellulis rotundatis pellucidis interstitiis grossis obscuris areolata.
—*L. Wightii*, Indiæ orientalis similis, sed paululum majora, foliis e cellulis grossioribus areolata
14 *L arrectifolia* (sp nov.), Mitt ; exilis; caulis repens, prostratus, folia assurgentia, ovali-oblonga, obtusa,
lobulo satis magno saccato , amphigastria nulla ; folia involucralia minora, lobulo unidentato ; perianthium
obovatum clavatumve, quinque-angulatum —Isle of Pines, ad folia *Spiridentis* adhærens (Strange!),
Samoa, in frondibus *Trichomanis repens* (Powell!). 15. *L rarifolia* (sp nov.), Mitt , caulis horizontalis, repens, cæspitosus, folia heteromorpha, assurgentia, rotunda obovatave, lobulo oblongo inflexo
planove, sæpe obsoleto, amphigastria nulla, folia involucralia majora, rotunda; perianthium pyriformi-
clavatum, obtusum, superne æqualiter pentangulum.—Samoa, ad corticem repens (Powell!) —Caulis brevissimus, cum foliis ¼ lineam latus. Folia olivaceo-fusca.—Species minuta, ramulis nonnullis, foliis assurgentibus, lobulo obsoleto, *Jungermanniæ parvæ* integrifoliæ simulans 16. *L alternifolia* (sp. nov), Mitt ,
caulis repens, ramosus , folia remotiuscula, alternantia, rotundata, obtusissima, lobulo totam marginis ventralis occupante dimidium folii æquante subovato tumido, apice unidentato, amphigastria obsoleta, folia
involucralia rotundata, lobulo acuto longe in caulem descendente, amphigastrium ovale, bifidum ; perianthium ovale, obtusum, compressum, dorso planum uni-ventre bicarinatum —Isle of Pines, ad folia *Spiridentis*
repens (Strange!) —Exilissima, ramis semilineam longis, foliis nudo oculo inconspicuis pallide viridibus,
cellulis minutis areolatis. 17 *L lancifolia* (sp nov), Mitt ; exilissima, caulis elongatus , folia alterna,
patentia, lanceolato-ovata, acuta, lobulo dimidium folii occupante obsoletove, amphigastria nulla; folia
involucralia brevia, amphigastriumque oblongum, bidentatum , perianthium ovale, apiculatum, compressum,
dorso uni- ventre biplicatum —Samoa, ad folia *Gaiotagliæ Samoanæ* repens (Powell) —Caulis 3-5 lineas
longus, tenuissimus Folia inter se remota, minutissima, pallide albo-viridia 18 *L. occulata*, Gottsche,
Lindenb et Nees Syn Hepat p 357 —Hawaii, ad *Radulam Javanicam* —This species received its name
from the presence of two or three enlarged hyaline cells so placed as to appear like an eyelet in the leaf
near to the stem 19. *L microdonta*, Gottsche, Lindenb. et Nees Syn Hepat p 337.—Hawaii, ad *Radulam
Javanicam*. 20 *L crenulata* (sp. nov.), Mitt ; caulis procumbens, ramosus , folia imbricata, rotunda,
crenata, lobulo parvo ovato involuto obsoletove ; amphigastria parva, subrotunda, bidentata; folia involucralia
obtusa obtuse acutave , amphigastrium oblongum ; perianthium obovatum, obtusum, compressum, dorso uni-
ventre biplicatum, angulis crenatis —Samoa, inter muscos late cæspitans (Powell!).—Caulis 3-6 lineas

3 H 2

longus, cum foliis ⅓ lineam latus Folia viridia subfuscaque, cellulis grossiusculis interstitiis crassis obscuris areolata.—*L vesicatæ* similis, foliis autem crenatis. 21. *L retusula* (sp. nov), Mitt , caulis exilis, prostratus; folia alterna, patentia, ovali-oblonga ovatave, apice rotundato, lobulo parvo ovato, margine ubique erosa, cellulis in papillam dentiformem producta areolata , amphigastria nulla , folia involucralia lobulo lato acuto , perianthium obovatum, retusum, compressum, dorso concavum, ventre biplicatum, plicis erosis —Aneitum, ad filicem quandam (Milne!)—Caulis cum foliis ⅓ lineam latus. Folia albo-viridia —*L. papillatæ* Mitt, e Nova Zelandia, similis, papillis autem multo humilioribus. 22 *L pentagona* (sp nov). Mitt ; caulis brevissimus , folia patentia, laxe imbricata, subovali-oblonga, crenata; amphigastria nulla , folia involucralia minora; perianthium obovatum, tumidum, obtuse quinque-angulatum, angulis crenatis —Samoa, ad frondes *Trichomanis* (Powell!) —Caulis cum foliis ⅓ lineam latus Folia albido-viridia 23 *L uncinata* (sp nov), Mitt.; caulis repens, ramosus; folia alterna, patentia, subovato-lanceolata, uncinata, decurva, acuta, e cellulis prominulis areolata, margine dorsali dentibus 1–4 plus minus conspicuis interdum obsoletis armata, ventrali integerrima, lobulo magno ovato tumido involuto, amphigastria parva, turcata , folia involucralia amphigastriumque spinuloso-dentata, ad perianthium obovatum obtuse pentangulum lævem appressa —Samoa, ad basin caulium *Syrrhopodontis crocei* (Powell), Sandwich Islands, ad caules *Mastigobryi cordistipuli* repens (Gaudichaud) —Caulis 3–6 lineas longus, latitudine cum foliis ⅓ lineam metiens Folia fusco-olivacea, involucralia adeo ad perianthium appressa ut primo adspectu facile prætervisa —*L hamatifoliæ* similis, perianthio autem lævi, et foliis magis hamatis divisa. 24 *L subquadrata* (sp nov), Mitt ; caulis repens, ramosus ; folia alternata, patentia, assurgentia, subquadrata, acutæ, inflexa, margine dorsali bi-tridentata, ventrale apicem versus uni-bidentata, lobulo magno ovato obsoletove, cellulis conformibus lævibus areolata , amphigastria ad basin usque in lacinias angustis fissa , folia involucralia amphigastriumque ovalia, apice bifido dentata; perianthium obconicum, angulis acutis dentatis —Samoa, ad frondes *Trichomanis* (Powell).—Caulis 3–4 lineas longus Folia minutissima 25. *L lævis* (sp nov), Mitt , caulis repens, ramosus; folia patentia, laxe imbricata, ovato-lanceolata, margine dorsali ventralique denticulis paucis brevibus distantibus serrata, cellulis lævibus areolata, lobulo ovato involuto tumido , amphigastria furcata, laciniis angustis —South Sea Islands (Nightingale) —*L uncinatæ* statura habituque simillima, foliis autem margine ventrali dentatis e cellulis lævibus areolatis

6. L. polyantha (sp. nov.), Mitt.; caulis prostratus, ramosus; folia divaricata, ovata, obtusa, lobulo parvo involuto; amphigastria parva, ad medium bifida ; folia involucralia subacuta, lobulo elongato acuto; perianthium obcordatum, compressum, dorso planum, ventre biplicatum, lateribus integerrimis subdenticulatisve , spicæ masculæ elongatæ, foliis imbricatis, margine cellulis majoribus limbatis —Viti, ad frondem *Trichomanis* (Harvey!), Aneitum, ad frondem filici repens (Strange), Samoa, in *Trichomanis* frondibus (Powell).

Caulis parvulus latitudine, cum foliis ⅓ lineam metiens. Folia pallida

7. L. convexifolia, (sp nov) Mitt.; caulis ramosus; folia divergentia, imbricata, ovali-oblonga, dorso convexa, obtusa, lobulo elongato involuto, usque ad medium marginis ventralis producto, apice dente calcariformi hamato; amphigastria parva, orbiculata, sinu parvo angustissimo bifida; folia involucralia conformia; amphigastrium oblongum, apice breviter bidentatum ; perianthium obovatum, obtusum, compressum, dorso uni- ventre biplicatum.—Viti (Seemann!), Pacific Islands (Nightingale), Samoa (Powell!).

Caulis vix unciam longus, cum foliis ⅓ lineam latus. Folia albo-viridia, firma, cellulis parvis rotundis areolata —*L. firmæ,* Mitt , Indiæ orientalis similis, sed minor et lobulis foliorum apice calcaratis.

8 L. superba, Mont. Cent. vol vi n. 5. t. 6 f. 2; Syll. p 83; caulis prostratus, ramosus; folia patula, semiorbiculata, apice in cucullum obtusum vel acutum tumidum producta, margine ventrali recto per longitudinem totam involuta, cellulis prominulis crenata vel lævis, dorsali 3–5-dentata, recta flexuosave, e cellulis rotundatis mollibus parietibus torvuloso-constrictis areolata; amphigastria duplicata, ad basin fere in lacinias angustis divergentibus fissa; folia involucralia minora, ovalia, integra, carina parva, crenata; perianthium oblongum, apice truncatum, compressum, dorso planum, ventre uni- vel inæqualiter biplicatum, angulis apice acutis obtusiusculisve crenatis.—Tahiti, in *Neckeria cylindracea* parasitans (Lepine), Samoa, ad filices sparsim repens (Powell), Viti (Seemann!).

Caulis 2–3 lineas longus Folia ⅓ lineam longa, pallide fusco-viridia —*L calyptrifoliæ* similis, sed major

IX. **Frullania,** Raddi, Gottsche, Lindenb. et Nees Syn. Hepat. p. 408. Caulis pinnatus, rarius dichotomus. Folia parva, rotundata, lobo ventrali sæpe parvo galeiformi vel clavato inflato, rarius explanato a cauli discreto, licinula parva dentiformi interdum interposita. Amphigastria rotundata, bifida, rarissime integra. Perianthium læve aut plicatum

The following are non-Vitian Polynesian species. viz. —1. *F Hutchinsiæ*, Hook Brit Jung t. 1 (*Jungermannia*) —Sandwich Islands (Tolmie), Samoa (Powell!), Tutuila (Veitch). 2 *F hypoleuca*, Nees ab E , Gottsche, Lindenb et Nees Syn Hepat p. 443 —Hawaii (Meyen; Herb Nees ab L), Sandwich Islands (Gaudichaud). 3 *F explicata*, Mont Ann. des Sc. Nat. 1843, p 256; Gottsche, Lindenb et Nees Syn. Hepat p 452 —Sandwich Islands (Gaudichaud) 4. *F. Meyeniana*, Lindenb. , Gottsche, Lindenb et Nees Syn Hepat. p 155 —Hawaii (Meyen; Herb. Nees ab L.). 5. *F oceanica* (sp nov.). Mitt , caulis pinnatus; folia divergentia, orbiculari-ovata, apiculo incurvo mucronata, lobulo a cauli distante clavato subpatente; amphigastria cordato-orbiculata, bifida, folia involucralia lobulis amphigastrioque laciniis lanceolato-subulatis subintegerrimis, perianthium oblongum, mucronatum, dorso planum, ventre unicarinatum —Hawaii (Beechey; Macrae), Sandwich Islands (Hillebrand), Samoa (Powell) — *F. Pacifica* robustior, intensius colorata, subnigra 6 *F. squarrosa*, Nees ab E , Gottsche, Lindenb. et Nees Syn Hepat. p 446 —Sandwich Islands (Hillebrand, n 13, ex parte) 7. *F. alolotis*, Nees ab E , Gottsche, Lindenb et Nees Syn Hepat p 447 —Lord Howe's Island (Milne!) 8. *F. pusilla* (sp nov). Mitt ; caulis procumbens, inordinatim pinnatus, folia divergentia, ovato-rotunda, obtusa, lobulo magno galeato decurvo, apice intra folii marginem descendente, amphigastria cuneato-rotunda, sinu parvo bifida, folia involucralia obtusa, lobulis binis lanceolatis margine undulatis; amphigastrium profunde bifidum, laciniis lanceolatis subdentatis, perianthium breve, obovatum, dorso planum, ventre uniplicatum, inferne tota superficie laciniis obtectum, apice nudum.—Isle of Pines, Main Peak (Milne!) —Caulis semunciam longus, cum foliis semilineam latus Folia fusca —*F alolotis* similis, sed lobulo majore. 9. *F Gaudichaudii*, Nees et Mont , Gottsche, Lindenb et Nees Syn Hepat p 135 —*Jubula Gaudichaudi*, Nees et Mont Ann des Sc Nat. 1836, cum icone f 2 —Aneitum (Milne) 10 *F. intermedia*, Nees ab E , Gottsche, Lindenb et Nees Syn Hepat. p 434 —Solomon Islands (Milne), Samoa, Manua, near the mountain Olotane (2000 ft) (Powell, n 11), Aneitum (Knight, n 159). 11. *F. angulosa* (sp. nov); caulis subpinnatus; folia explanata, divergentia, orbiculato-ovalia, apice anguloso-subdentato, lobulo parvo, cauli approximato dependente anguste lanceolato explanato, in ramulis ulterioribus parva, obovata, inflata, decurvata, amphigastria patentia, orbiculato-ovata, sinu latiusculo, laciniis acuminatis; folia involucralia oblonga, lobulo amphigastrioque quadripartito serrata; perianthium ovale, triplicatum, plicis sublævibus — Samoa (Powell) —Caulis 4-5 uncias longus, ramis uncialibus Folia viridia —*F. nodulosa* et *F. intermedia* gracilior.

1. **F. trichodes,** Mitt. Bonplandia, 1862, p. 19; caulis elongatus, gracilis, pinnatus; folia subremota, patentia, ovali-orbiculata, obtusa, concava, ramea angustiora, margine angulis parvis irregulari implana, cellulis omnibus oblongis, lobulo clavato cauli parallelo vel paululum declinato interdum evoluto; amphigastria suboblonga, incurva, inferne marginibus sinuato-recurvis, apice bifidis, sinu angusto, laciniis latiusculis, folia amphigastriumque involucrale spinuloso-dentata.—Viti (Seemann!), on the branches or stems of *Garovaglia setigera*, n. 816.

Caulis 4-uncialis, ramis 2-3 lineas longis —*F. pacifica* gracilior Folia involucrum versus plura dentata.

2. **F. pacifica,** Tayl. Lond Journ. Bot 1846, p. 406; caulis elongatus, gracilis, ramis breviusculis, pinnatus; folia divergentia, ovata, breviter apiculata, apiculo incurvo, lobulo clavato a cauli remoto parallelo lacinia parva interjecta vel evoluto lanceolato incurvo; amphigastria orbiculata, bifida; folia involucralia lobis lanceolatis acuminatis integerrimis; perianthium oblongum, trigonum, mucronatum.—Pacific Islands (Nightingale), Samoa, Manua, near the mountain Olotane (2000 ft) (Powell, n. 14), Viti (Seemann).

Caules biunciales, ramis sesquilineam longis, cum foliis ¼ lineam lati

3. **F. meteoroides,** Mitt Bonplandia, 1862, p. 19; caulis elongatus, gracilis, pinnatus bipinnatusque; folia caulina ovali-orbiculata, paululum devexa, apice incurva involutave rotundata, apiculo minuto subobsoleto terminata, lobulo evoluto lanceolato erecto, cauli approximato, in ramis cylindrico

subclavato erecto subdeclinatove a cauli remotiore; amphigastria suborbiculata, bifida, sinu laciniisque acutis; folia involucralia longiora, late lanceolata, lobulis late ovato-lanceolatis, amphigastrioque dentato-laceris; perianthium emergens oblongum, obtusum, apiculatum, dorso lævi ventre unicarinatum.—Viti (Seemann ! n. 834; Milne).

4. **F. vaga,** (sp. nov.) Mitt.; caulis procumbens, subpinnatim divisus; folia divaricata, oblongo-rotundata, apice inflexa, lobulo cauli approximato hamato decurvato; amphigastria rotunda, transversim paululo latiora, apice sinu parvo brevissime fissa, lobulum tegentia —Viti (Seemann !).

Caulis biuncialis, cum foliis sublineam latus Folia castanea.

5. **F. nodulosa,** Nees ab E.; Gottsche, Lindenb. et Nees Syn. Hepat p 443; caulis, ramis elongatis divergentibus, pinnatus bipinnatusve, ramosus; folia divergentia, orbiculata, margine apice ventralique inflexa, lobulo parvo cauli approximato claviformi dependente, amphigastria orbicularia, basi cordata, medio carinata, apice sinu parvo rectangulari bidentata, margine recurva; folia involucralia, marginibus incurvis subintegerrimis; amphigastrium lacero-serratum, perianthium ovatum, dorso convexum, ventre unicarinatum, angulis subdentatis — Viti (Seemann !), Tahiti (Menzies !).

6. **F. deflexa,** Mitt. Bonplandia, 1862, p. 19, caulis elongatus, bipinnatus, folia orbiculata, obtusa, lobulo clavato vel pyriformi deflexo a cauli subremoto, amphigastria magna, lobulum tegentia, oblata, emarginata, sinu laciniisque obtusiusculis.—Viti (Seemann ! n. 834).

Caulis 4-5 uncias longus, ramis divaricatis subuncialibus —*F intermediæ* statura similis, folia autem *F nodulosæ* similiora sed magis orbiculata, et lobulo a cauli remotiore —Spicæ masculæ breves, foliis arcte imbricatis

X. Marsupidium, Mitt. in Hooker, Handb of the New Zealand Flora, p 751 et 753 Caules erecti ascendentesve, simplices. Folia subverticalia. Amphigastria nulla. Perianthium in ramo brevi basilari nudum.

1. **M. Urvilleanum,** Mont. (*Scapania*); Gottsche, Lindenb. et Nees Syn. Hepat. 63, folia patentia, rotunda, apice integra vel oblique subretusa, denticulata, cellulis parvis rotundatis areolata. —Viti (Seemann).

A single stem picked from amongst Mosses is all that indicates the presence of this or some closely-allied species.

XI. Metzgeria, Raddi. Frons tenuis, furcata pinnatimve divisa, costa angusta percursa, e latere ventrali fructifera. Flores masculi in lobulis excavatis inclusi, e latere ventrali costæ oriundi.

1. **M. furcata,** Linn. Sp. Plant. (*Jungermannia*); frons furcata, vage divisa, linearis, pagina superiore glabra, margine costaque paginæ inferioris setulosa vel denudata, involucro e costa oriundo parvo monophyllo, calyptra carnosula setulosa.—Viti (Seemann), Samoa (Powell, n 164).

Frondes in speciminibus Samoanis margine recurvæ serie duplici ciliorum fimbriatæ, forma communi Europææ omnino similia.

XII. Sarcomitrium, Corda in Sturm Flora Germ. vol. ii. p. 120. t. 33. Frons subsimplex, pinnata bipinnatave, e costa valida carnosa fere totam occupante constituta. Fructus lateralis. Flores masculi in lobis propriis dispositi, antheridiis immersis.—*Aneura* et *Metzgeria* ex parte, Gottsche, Lindenb. et Nees, Syn. Hepat. p. 493 et 501.

The following is a non-Vitian species —1 *S multifidum,* Linn Sp Pl (*Jungermannia*) —Samoa (Powell !) n. 145).

1. **S. plumosum,** Mitt. Bonplandia, 1862, p. 19; caulis ascendens, compressus, nudus, bipinnatus, ramis ambitu late ovatis ramulis compressis margine integerrimis pellucidis nervo paululo obscuriore notatis; involucri squamæ dactyloideæ.—Viti (Seemann ! n. 847).

Ordo CX. MARCHANTIEÆ.

(Auctore W. Mitten.)

The following are non-Vitian genera, viz :—

I. Dumortiera, Reinw Blume et Nees, Gottsche, Lindenb et Nees Syn Hepat. p 512

1. *D trichocephala*, Nees, Hook Icon. pl 2. t. 159—Sandwich Islands (Douglas, n 71, Hillebrand, n. 4), Samoa (Powell, n 150).

II. Dendroceros, Nees ab E , Gottsche, Lindenb. et Nees Syn Hepat p. 570

1. *D. granulatus* (sp nov), Mitt , frons subpinnatim ramosa, costa crassa opaca, limbo marginali lato margine dentato valde flexuoso crispatoque e cellulis subpellucidis areolato; involucrum elongatum, tuberculosum ; capsula elongata, asperula —Samoa (Powell, n 114) —Frondes unciam longi, sesquilineam lati, rubiginosi —In this species the thin border of the frond is so much sinuated and crisped that the nerve appears as if beset with lobe-like leaves 2 *D tumidulus* (sp nov), Mitt ; frons furcatim ramosa, costa crassiore obscuriore e cellulis elongatis laxis areolata, limbo plicato tumido sinuato margine subdentato cellulis granuloso-obscuris rotundis areolato, involucrum elongatum, læve, capsula punctulata.—Samoa ad muscos repens (Powell) —Frondes lineam latæ, virides ; involucra bilinearia ; capsula æquilonga —This has the lamina bordering the fronds very little sinuated and the central costa far more soft and insensibly passing into the margin

III. Anthoceros, Micheli ; Gottsche, Lindenb. et Nees Syn. Hepat. p. 582

1. *A flagellaris* (sp nov.), Mitt , frons sinuata, lobata, planiuscula, ecostata, lævis, margine ramis ascendentibus elongatis angustis furcatis compressis obscurius areolatis ramosa ; involucrum læve, capsula elongata exserta, valvis divisis flexuosis —Samoa, on decayed bark (Powell) —*A. lævi* Europæ similis, sed prolongationibus 4-6 lineas longis singularis —The curious branches which arise from the edges of the fronds much resemble in appearance some forms of *Pellia*. Two very different-looking specimens of species of *Plagiochasma* have been received from the Pacific, but too incomplete to afford any safe distinctive characters.

I. Marchantia, Linn Receptaculum fœmineum masculumque ex apice frondis productum, margine radiatum. Involucra fœminea radiis alterna. Perianthia 4–5-fida. Gemmæ in scyphis e dorso frondis enatis impositæ.

1. **M. nitida**, Lehm. et Lindenb ; Gottsche, Lindenb et Nees Syn. Hepat. p. 532 ; frondes elongatæ, planiusculæ, læves, poris parvis notatæ, subtus purpureæ, squamis parvis nervo contiguis ; receptaculum fœmineum in pedunculo ramentoso hemisphæricum, subintegrum, margine brevissime lobatum, subtus ramentis dense obsitum ; receptaculum masculum lobatum.—Viti Levu (Græffe), Samoa, Manua (1400 ft.), (Powell, n 147), Tahiti (Collie), Hawaii (Macrae), Sandwich Islands (Hillebrand).

The specimens of this *Marchantia* are none of them sufficient for an exact determination, but they appear to be the same as the species found in New Zealand as well as in India

Ordo CXI. LICHENES.

(Auctore J. M. Crombie.)

There can be little doubt that Viti, if not particularly rich in Lichens, must yet afford a fair proportion of subtropical species It is, however, to be regretted that the few botanical collectors who have visited it have here, as in other similar regions, paid so little attention to this interesting class of cryptogams. A few of the larger corticole species, chiefly *Stictas*, alone appear in herbaria, while terricole and saxicole species are entirely neglected Dr Nylander's Synopsis of the Lichens of the neighbouring Island of New Caledonia, amounting to 220 species (exclusive of varieties), will serve to give some idea of those which may be expected to occur also in Viti, and to show that a rich harvest awaits the researches of future collectors throughout the extensive Polynesian group.

In Forster's herbarium there are the following Lichens from Polynesia, but all without exact localities —3 *Lichen globiferus*, Linn Mant. 133, Prodr 586, C J A 383=*Sphærophoron coralloides*, Pers in
Ust N. Ann vol i p 23. 5 *L hirtus*, Linn Fl. Suec 1128, Prodr. 588, sed hoc specimen potius ut
videtur ad *U floridam*, Frs. L E. 18, referendum est 6 *L pulmonarius*, Linn. Fl. Suec 1087 *Sticta
pulmonacea*, Ach L N 449 *Pulmonaria reticulata*, Hoffm Pl. Lich t 1. f. 2 7 *Sticta aurata*, Ach.
Meth 277, non typica sed forma prope ad var *pallentem*, Nyl Syn 361. 8. *Lichen fragilis*, Linn=*Sphæro-
phoron compressum*, Ach Meth 135, et *S australe*, (Laur) Hook Antarct 195,530   10? *Platisma filix*,
Hoffm C J. A 387=*Stictina filicina*, Ach ut infra   11 *Lichen fucoides*, Linn, sed hoc specimen modo
Ramalina calicaris est

I. **Stictina,** Nyl.   Thallus frondosus, varie lobatus vel laciniatus, sæpe sorediferus, pagina
infera rhizinis simplicibus, cyphellis vel pseudo-cyphellis, strato gonimo e granulis gonimis glauco-
virescentibus vel glauco-cœrulescentibus constante.   Apothecia juvenilia receptaculo thallino
induta.

1. **S. quercizans,** Ach. Syn. 234, pro p Nyl. Syn p. 344; *Sticta cinchonæ*, Del. St. p. 155;
S. damæcornis, var. *Weigelii*, Ach L. U. 446; thallus cervino-fuscescens, mediocris, membranaceus,
nitidiusculus, lævis, laciniato-lobatus, lobis crenato-divisis, margine granulato-isidioso, undulato,
subtus tomentosus fuscescens, ambitu pallidus; apothecia submarginalia, fere mediocria, margine
tenui nudo; sporæ unicolores, 3-septatæ, fusiformes.—Viti (Seemann! n. 854).

II. **Sticta,** Ach.   Thallus ut in præcedente, sed stratum gonimon e gonidiis veris viridibus vel
flavo-viridibus compositum.   Cetera omnino sicut in *Stictina*.

1. **S. damæcornis,** var *caperata* (Borr. Herb), Nyl Syn. 357; *S. patula*, Mont. L. Jav 14;
thallus flavicans, firmior, late expansus, lævis, imbricato-lobatus, lobis apicalibus obtusis, flavicans,
subtus fusco-nigricans, ambitu cinereo-fuscescens, interdum cephalodiis glomerulosis leptogioideis;
apothecia fusco-rufa, mediocria, marginalia aut sparsa, margine thallino parce crenulato, sporæ
incolores, 1–3-septatæ, fusiformes —Viti (Seemann! n. 848).

2. **S. filicina,** Ach. Meth. 275, Nyl. Syn. 319; *Lichen filix*, Sw. Meth. Musc t. 2. f 1, *Platisma filix*, Hoffm. Pl. Lich. 3. t 55, thallus pallide cinereo-flavicans, mediocris, parum rigescens,
subopacus, lævis, substipitatus, lobis margine sinuoso, subtus ochraceo-pallidus, tomento rhizineo vix
ullo, apothecia badio-rufa, sparsa, mediocria, margine thallino pallidiore integro; sporæ incolores,
1–3-septatæ, fusiformes.—Viti (Seemann! n. 849).

3. **S. damæcornis,** Ach. Meth. 270, Nyl. Syn. 356; *Platisma cornudamæ*, Hoffm. Pl Lich.
t. 24. f. 1; *S. macrophylla*, Schær. Enum. 31; thallus pallide fusco-rufescens, late expansus, vix
rigescens, parum nitidiusculus, lævis, lineari-laciniatus, laciniis pinnatifidis apice dichotomis, subtus
ochraceo-pallescens, tomento rhizineo parco, apothecia fusco-rufa, præcipue marginalia, margine
thallino fere integro; sporæ incolores, 1–3-septatæ, fusiformes.—Viti (Seemann! n. 850).

III. **Ramalina,** Ach. Fries.   Thallus pallidus, compressus, non nihil rigescens, erectus vel
prostratus, laciniose divisus; apothecia sparsa vel marginalia; sporæ incolores, oblongæ, 1-septatæ;
paraphyses discretæ, mediocres.

1. **R. calicaris,** Fries, L. E 30, Nyl. Prodr. 47, et var. *canaliculata*, Fries, l. c., L. S. Exs. 72;
thallus pallidus, rigescens, compressus, linearis, lacunose inæqualis, varie divisus, parum canaliculatus;
apothecia subterminalia, pallida; sporæ curvatulæ vel rectiusculæ, 1-septatæ, incolores.—Nomen ver-
naculum Vitiense " Lami ni Vanua."   Viti (Seemann! n. 851).

IV. **Coccocarpia,** Pers.   Thallus typice monophyllus, textura cellulosa, granula gonima
exhibens.   Apothecia biatorina, adnata.   Sporæ 8-næ, incolores, simplices.

1. **C. molybdæa**, Pers in Gaud. Uran 206, Nyl. Lich. Nov. Calcd. p. 22; thallus glaucescens, lobatus, ambitu radiato-inciso, margine ambitus crenato, et versus ambitum concentrice arcuato-rugulosus, subtus nigricanti-rhizinosus; apothecia rufa, plana, mediocria; sporæ ellipsoides, simplices. (Specimen tamen in hoc herb. non bene est evolutum.)—Viti (Seemann! n. 852).

V. **Verrucaria**, Pers. Thallus varius, sæpe obsoletus, aut nullus proprius. Apothecia pyrenodinea, perithecio demigrato, raro pallida, rarius colorata; sporæ variæ. Spermogonia sterigmatibus simplicibus.

1. **V. aurantiaca**, Nyl. Syn. Pyren. p 48; *Pyrenula aurantiaca*, Fée, Ess. Suppl t. 37. f. 1; thallus tenuis, intense aurantiacus, lævis vel ruguloso-inæqualis, opacus, determinatus, intus albicans; apothecia innata, perithecio integro nigro, minuta, interdum quædam confluentia, sporæ incolores vel fuscæ, 4-loculares.—Growing on Cocoa-nut-trees, and imparting to their trunks a reddish hue (Seemann! n. 865).

Ordo CXII. FUNGI.

(Auctore Worthington G. Smith.)

But few Fungi were collected by Dr Seemann, and two of these were imperfect His n 856 is a species of *Lentinus*, allied to *L vulpinus*, Fr, but the materials are insufficient, whilst his n 857 belongs to *Rhizomorpha*, formerly held to be a good genus, but now known to be only the myceloid condition of different Fungi This *Rhizomorpha* is one of the few Fungi used for dress, and thus described in Dr Seemann's 'Viti,' p 352 Speaking of the different "Likus," or dresses, made of leaves and fibres, the author says —"Amongst the permanent Likus is one termed 'Sausauwai,' the long black fringes of which, playing on the white Tapa, or on the fine limbs of the natives, has a most graceful appearance Both on account of the scarcity of the materials of which it is composed, and its being unaffected by water, especially when greased with cocoa-nut oil, the Sausauwai is highly valued by fishermen, and all people living on the coast of Fiji, they will give twenty fathoms of white Tapa, and the Tonguese and Samoans as much as £1 sterling, for a single one of these elegant articles of dress The fringes of which it is composed are of the thickness of a common wire, rather flexible, and occasionally ornamented with small beads. Placed under the microscope, the vegetable origin of these fringes becomes at once evident, and they are found to be composed of glossy black joints, of unequal length None, save a few natives, had ever seen the plant producing them, and it was the general belief of all the foreign residents in Fiji that they were the roots of a certain tree, until Mr. Pritchard and myself made the subject a point of special inquiry during our first visit to Navua A few words from Chief Kuruduadua, and two large knives held out by us as a reward, induced two young men to procure a quantity of this singular production sufficient for scientific examination, proving it to be, not the root of a tree, as had been believed, but the entire body of a species of *Rhizomorpha* The plant is vernacularly termed 'Wa loa,' literally, black creeper, from *wa*, creeper, and *loa*, black—a name occasionally applied to the Liku made of it also The Wa loa is confined to the southwestern parts of Viti Levu, where it grows in swamps on decaying wood fallen to the ground, the threads of which it consists are several feet long, leafless, not much branched, and they are furnished here and there with little shield-like expansions, acting as suckers, by means of which the plant is attached to the dead wood upon which it grows. The threads, having been beaten between stones in order to free them from impurities adhering, are buried for two or three days in muddy places, and are then ready for plaiting them to the waistband."

I. **Agaricus**, Linn. Lamellæ membranaceæ, persistentes, acie acutæ, trama subfloccosa cum hymenophoro infero concretæ. Fungi carnosi, putrescentes nec exsiccati reviviscentes.

1. **A. (Pleurotus) pacificus**, Berk in Hook Journ. 1842, p. 451; pallide ochraceus, pileo apode, resupinato-reflexo, orbiculari, deinde in lobos pileiformes fisso, tenui, glabro, subvirgato, margine obscuriore elegantissime e lamellis tenuibus postice acutis integerrimis striato.—On sticks covered with bark, Viti Islands (R. B. Hinds!).

Allied to *A. nidulans.*

II. **Schizophyllum,** Fr. Fungus excarnis, aridus Lamellæ coriaceæ, ramoso-flabelliformes, acie longitudinaliter fissæ, lamellulis discretis extrorsum revolutis patulisque —Fr. Epicr. p. 402.

1. **S. commune,** Fr. Epicr. p. 403; pileo postice adnato, subporrecto, simplici lobatoque; lamellis e grisco fusco-purpurascentibus villosis, acie revolutis —Viti Islands (R. B. Hinds!).

III **Polyporus,** Fr. Hymenophorum inter poros in tramam descendens, sed cum eisdem in stratum proprium seu discolor mutatum —Fr. Epicr. p. 427.

1. **P. sanguineus,** Fr. Epicr. p 444; sanguineo-miniatus; pileo coriaceo, tenui, reniformi, glabro, nitido, stipite laterali brevi, basi orbiculari dilatata adnato; poris minutis, rotundis —Viti (Seemann! n. 857).

2. **P. affinis,** Fr. Epicr. p. 445; pileo papyraceo, flabelliformi, rigido, castaneo, zonis obscurioribus picto, stipiteque laterali tenui æquali castaneo-fusco, basi scutato-adnato, glabris; poris determinatis, curtis, minimis, albo-alutaceis —P. *lateralis,* Pers —Viti (Seemann! n. 858).

3. **P. hirsutus,** Fr. Epicr. p 477; pileo suberoso-coriaceo, convexo-plano, pilis rigidis hirtosulcis concentricis zonato, unicolori, albido; poris rotundis, obtusis, albidis, fuscescentibus.—Viti (Seemann! n. 859).

IV. **Xylaria,** Fr. Mycelium atrum (exsertum saltem), matrici sæpe maculatæ vel marmoratæ innatum. Stroma lignoso-suberinum, rarius carnosum, extus sæpissime atro-fuligineum, quandoque tamen lætius coloratum, cylindricum, clavatum, aut filiforme, teres seu compressum, simplex vel in ramos varie discedens indeque quasi fruticulosum. Conidia minima, ovata vel lanceolata, summam stromatis recentis partem in qua nascuntur veluti pulvere candido ("velo farinaceo, heterogeneo") cinereo, ærugineo luteove obruentia, moxque vel tardius evanida; hymenio conidiophoro, gongylis concolore, e sterigmatibus cylindricis brevibus simplicibus et stipatissime sociatis facto, aliquandoque in squamas tandem secedente, stromate nudato nigricante aut varie infuscato Perithecia exigua, globosa, brevissime rostrata, aterrima, in extimo stromatis strato spisse nidulantia et modice protuberantia; parietibus crustaceis; nucleo maturo udo, fluxili, atro. Thecæ anguste lineares, deorsum versus breviter attenuatæ, 8-sporæ et paraphysibus longe filiformibus simplicibusque stipatæ Sporæ obliqque monostichæ, ovatæ, plus minus inæquilaterales, læves, atræ, uniloculares oleoque fetæ.—Tul. Carp. vol. ii. p. 4.

1. **X. Feejeensis,** Berk. in List of Seemann's Viti Plants; suberosa, simplex vel sursum palmata, fusco-purpurea, rugosa, rimulosa; perithecis minutis, subglobosis, subprominulis, ostiolis nigris; stipite brevi vel nullo.—*Sphæria (Hypoxylon) Feejeensis,* Berk in Hook. Journ. 1842, p. 456.—On stumps, Viti Islands (R. B. Hinds).

More nearly allied to *Xylaria hypoxylon,* Grev., than *X polymorpha,* Grev., the nearest ally being *Hypoxylon scruposum,* Mont

V. **Sphæria,** Pers Mycelium matrici plus minus maculatæ glabræque immissum, nec conspicue byssinum. Conceptacula dense gregaria, suffulcro natali imposita, exigua, globosa, nonnihil conica vel deformia, brevissime imo vix papillata, atque ex parietibus glabris atris et duris facta; alia minora pycnidea, stylosporis rectis et spermatiomorphis, scilicet brevissime linearibus et exilissimis feta; alia ascophora, thecis lineari-cylindricis monostiche octosporis, sporis autem ovatooblongis multipartitis fuscis muticis et nudis gravida.—Tul. Carp. vol. ii. p. 244.

1. **S. transversalis**, Schw. in Fr. El. vol. ii. p. 91, innata, perithcciis erumpentibus astomis glabris, demum basi circumscissis, ramento macula fusca; sporidia uniseriata, fusca, elliptica, subglobosa v. globosa, 0·0004 unc long. (fide Currey in Linn. Trans vol. xxii. p. 328).—*Hoomospora transversalis*, Breb. ex Berk.—Summit of Taviuni Island (Seemann ! n. 860).

Dr Seemann thus describes in his 'Viti,' p. 28, the occurrence of this plant on Taviuni Island — "After another hour's scramble we reached the summit, and found it to all appearance a large extinct crater filled with water, and on the north-eastern part covered with a vegetable mass, so much resembling in colour and appearance the green fat of the turtle, as to have given rise to the popular belief that the fat of all the turtles eaten in Fiji is transported hither by supernatural agency, which is stated to be the reason why on the morning after a turtle-feast the natives always feel very hungry. This jelly-like mass is several feet thick, and entirely composed of some microscopic cryptogams, which, from specimens I submitted to the Rev M J Berkeley, a weighty authority in these matters, proved to be *Hoomospora transversalis* of Brebisson, and the representative of quite a new genus, named *Hoomonema fluitans*, Berkl. A tall species of sedge was growing among them, and gave some degree of consistency to the singular body. We were not aware until it was too late that these strange productions were only floating on the top of the lake and forming a kind of crust, or else we should not have ventured upon it. On the contrary, we took it to be part of a swamp, that might be safely crossed, though not without difficulty, for we were always up to our knees, often to our hips, in this jelly. All this caused a great deal of merriment. A little hunchback, who carried a basket swinging on a stick, looked most ludicrous in his endeavours to keep pace with us. Now and then, when one or the other was trying to save himself from sinking into inextricable positions, he had to crawl like a reptile, and the others were not slow to laugh at his expense. The first symptoms of danger were several large fissures which occurred in the crust we were wading through. The water in them was perfectly clear, and a line of many yards let down reached no bottom. These fissures became more and more numerous as we advanced, until the vegetable mass abruptly terminated in a lake of limpid water full of eels. The border was rather more solid than the mass left behind, and all sat down to rest, from the great exertion it had required to drag ourselves for more than a mile and a half through one of the worst swamps I ever crossed."

Ordo EQUISETACEÆ.

Milde, in his 'Monographia Equisetorum' (Dresden, 1865), which was published in the Nova Acta, vol xxii, advocates the division of *Equisetum* into two genera, which he names respectively *Equisetum* and *Hippochæte*, and of which he publishes generic characters; but in his subsequent enumeration of the species he abstains from adopting his new genus, and leaves it to future botanists to resume the responsibility of changing so many long-established names. Milde deals exclusively with the recent members of the Order *Equisetaceæ*; but Carruthers (Seem Journ of Bot. vol. v. p. 349. t. 70) has worked out the fossil ones, and, according to his able researches, the whole Order, as far as at present known, is composed of two genera, viz *Calamites* (including *Asterophyllites, Annularia, Sphenophyllum*) and *Equisetum*. Carruthers's researches throw quite a new light upon the nature of our present *Equisetaceæ*,—the sheath, for instance, surrounding the stem being proved beyond doubt to be nothing but a whorl of leaves, very much reduced and united by their edges. In fact, the *Equisetaceæ*, as they are now growing on the globe, are but inferior *Calamites*, and fully bear out Gœppert's dictum, that Darwinism derives no support whatsoever from the results of fossil botany.

I. **Hippochæte**, Milde, Monogr. Equiset. p. 379. Stomata 2, series maxime regulares in valleculis efformantia, semper stricte verticillata posita, in depressione profunda epidermidis sita, singula cellula quarta a se invicem disjuncta. Stoma exterius lamina silicea continua foramine amplo irregulariter pertuso obtectum. Radii stomatis exterioris numerosi 16–21, primum paralleli, demique divergentes, rarius furcati. Annuli incrassati, in caule veri desunt. Ocreola atro-fusca, fragilis, ex parte v. omnino velata, et chorophyllo stomatibus et fasciculis semper destituta videtur. Rami lacuna centrali præditi. Primum ramorum internodium vagina caulina semper brevius. Spica apiculata. Rhizoma tuberculis siliceis exasperatum. Plantæ caulibus homomorphis instructæ.—

Equisetum, Amb. *Equiseta hiemalia*, A. Braun. *Equiseta stichopora*, A Braun. *Equiseta cryptopora*, Milde. *Sclerocaulon*, Doll.

1. **H. debilis,** Seem.; caulis sublævis, leviter sulcatus, debilis, carinæ 8–32 et complures valleculis multo angustiores; vaginæ cylindricæ, truncatæ v. fragmentis dentium vestitæ, breves, longiores quam latæ, ore paulum v. non ampliato, foliola subplana; carina media angulata sub vaginæ margine evanescente et lineis tuberculorum plus minus exsertis singulis marginalibus; dentibus lanceolato-subulatis medio atro-fuscis membranaceis 2–4-nis basi et sub apice connatis plerumque truncatis; rami 1–4-ni, irregulariter dispositi, 8–∞-anguli, cauli simillimi. Epidermidis lumen amplum; cellulæ undulatæ, stomatum cryptop series 1-lineatæ 6 et compluribus cellulis interpositis, carinæ convexæ nudæ v. fasciis, valleculæ plerumque rosulis vestitæ; lacuna centralis ¼ et amplior, valleculares magnæ oblongæ —*Equisetum debile*, Roxb mss. ex Vauch. Monogr. Preles. (Mem. Soc. Phys. et Hist. Nat. Gen. vol. i. p. 387); Milde, Monogr. l. c. p. 477. n. 17. *E. aquaticum*, Noronh. Verb. Bat. Gen. vol. v. (1790) p. 14? *E. Timorianum*, Vauch. l. c. p. 376. *E. palleus*, Wall. Cat. n. 1037. *E. laxum*, Blume, Enum. Pl. Jav. p. 274. *E. virgatum*, Blume, l. c. p. 274. *E. elongatum*, Mett. in Ann. Sc. Nat. ser. 4. tome iv. (1861) p. 87. *E hiemale*, Mett. in Pl. Ind. Or. edid. Hohenacker, n. 1240. *E. Huegelii*, Milde in Verhandl. Zool. Bot. Gesell. Wien, 1861, p. 356. Nomen vernac. Vitiense, "Masi ni tabua"—Growing socially and in great abundance on low swampy banks of the river Navua, Island of Viti Levu (Seemann! n. 697). Also collected at Aneitum, New Hebrides (Milne and M'Gillivray!), and New Caledonia (Vieillard!), and Japan. Widely diffused over tropical Asia and the Archipelago.

The Vitian native name, "Masi ni tabua," of this plant relates to its use of polishing whales' teeth (tabua) with it "Masi" is also the name of a wild Fig (*F scabra*), the rough leaves of which are used (as are those of the Sandpaper-tree (*Curatella*) in tropical America) for polishing and scouring things

No *Equisetum* has as yet been found in New Holland, but until recently it was not known that *E. debile* existed in the Polynesian Islands, and it is very probable that, like many other Asiatic types, it may also be found on the continent of Australia.

ADDITIONS AND CORRECTIONS.

———•———

CRUCIFERÆ.

Cardamine sarmentosa, Forst. Supra, p. 5.—Viti, locality not specified (Harvey! in Mus. Brit.).

PITTOSPOREÆ.

Pittosporum rhytidocarpum, A. Gray. Supra, p. 8.—Nadi, Island of Vanua Levu (Harvey! in Mus. Brit.).

TERNSTRŒMIACEÆ.

Eurya angustifolia, Blume. Supra, p. 14 —Viti, locality not specified (Harvey! in Mus. Brit.).

Saurauja rubicunda, Seem. Supra, p. 14 —Nadi, Island of Vanua Levu (Harvey !).

Trimenia, (gen. nov.) Seem. Flores polygami. Sepala 5, inæqualia, imbricata, a bracteolis ad petala subgradatim aucta. Petala 5, valde imbricata. Stamina 10, 2-seriata; filamenta brevissima; antheræ lineares, erectæ, basifixæ, connectivo inappendiculato, longitudinaliter dehiscentes. Ovarium . . . .—Arbor glabra; foliis oppositis, ovato-lanceolatis, acuminatis, serratis, basi in petiolum attenuatis, coriaceis, glabris, penninerviis; floribus brunneis, minutis, in paniculas axillares dispositis.

I have named this new genus in honour of my friend Dr Henry Trimen, of the British Museum, author (with Mr T. Dyer) of a 'Flora of Middlesex,' and several valuable botanical papers *Trimenia* will have to be placed in the tribe of *Ternstrœmieæ* of Bentham and Hooker, though the panicles are pluriflorous There is only one species known, viz —

1. **T. weinmanniæfolia,** (sp nov) Seem. (Tab. XCIX.)—*Weinmannia* sp., Seem. in Bonpl. 1861, p. 256.—Island of Kadavu (Seemann! n. 198)

In habit this singular plant is so very much like some species of *Weinmannia* that in my preliminary List of Vitian Plants, published in the 'Bonplandia,' I enumerated it as one, and only became aware of my error when I worked up the Order of *Saxifrageæ* for this 'Flora.' The branches are straight and terete, the petioles ½ inch long; the blade of leaf 3-3½ inches long, and 6-9 lines broad, rather rugose The flowers (only the male being known) are arranged in axillary panicles, which are shorter than the leaves; they form, with the bracts and calyx, obovate bodies, scarcely attaining the size of peas. The petals are ovate-obtuse, and about a third larger than the stamens The filaments are slightly coherent at base, and the anthers covered with minute glands

EXPLANATION OF PLATE XCIX., representing *Trimenia weinmanniæfolia,* Seem —Fig 1, an entire male flower; 2, the same, with bracts, sepals, and some of the petals, removed, 3, a stamen:—*all magnified*

MALVACEÆ.

Gossypium tomentosum, Nutt. Supra, p. 22—Add: *G. religiosum*, A Gray, Bot. Wilkes, vol i p. 179 (non Cav.). *G. Sandwichense*, Parlat. Sp. Cot. p. 37. t. 6. f. B (1866); Seem Journ. of Bot. 1866, p. 268.

Gossypium religiosum, Linn. Supra, p. 22 in adn —Add: *G. Barbadense*, Hook. et Arn. Bot. Beech. p. 60. *G. Taitense*, Parlat. Sp Cot. p 39. t 6. f. A; Seem. Journ. of Bot. 1866, p 268

HUMIRIACEÆ. (Insert before *Malpighiaceæ*, p. 29.)

I. **Thacombauia,** (gen. nov) Seem. Sepala 5, imbricata. Petala . . . . Stamina basi in tubum brevem connata; . . . . Discus annularis, e squamis 5 clavatis compositus. Ovarium 5-loculare, apice 5-lobum; ovula in loculis 2 superposita. Drupa . . . .—Arbuscula glabra; ramis teretibus; foliis exstipulatis, alternis, brevipetiolatis, ovato-oblongis, acuminatis, grosse dentatis v. integerrimis, coriaceis, nitidis; floribus axillaribus, cymosis, minutis.

I have named this new genus after Ebenezer Thakombau (=Cacobau), King of Viti, under whose rule civilization took firm root in the islands on which this work treats, and who has shown himself most friendly to me during my stay in his dominions. The materials were sent to me after my departure by Mr Jacob Storck, and, though they are not perfect, are yet sufficient to show that this plant belongs to the Order *Humiriaceæ*, until now supposed not to be represented in Polynesia, of which it appears to constitute a new genus, differing from *Vantanea* and *Humiria* in the nature of the glandular disk, and from *Sacoglottis* both by the nature of the disk and its two-ovuled cells of ovary. At present there is only one species known, viz :—

1. **T. Vitiensis,** (sp. nov.) Seem (Tab. C.).—Viti Levu (Storck!)

Not unlike, in general appearance, *Casearia Melistaurum*, DC. (supra, p 98) Branches and leaves glabrous Petiole 6–12 lines long Blade of leaf from 8–12 inches long, and 4–5 inches broad, leathery Sepals ovate, obtuse or slightly pointed, pubescent on both sides. Staminal tube 5-lobed, the lobes alternating with 5 clavate glands Or, is what I have termed the staminal tube a glandular disk? In that case there would be a double disk, the inner terminating in 5 clavate glands, which would make the genus still more distinct from the others of the Order.

EXPLANATION OF PLATE C, representing *Thacombauia Vitiensis*, Seem.—Fig 1, a flower far advanced, and with stamens and petals fallen off; 2, the same, with the sepals bent back (N B There is here drawn one clavate gland too many); 3, one of the clavate glands; 4, longitudinal section of ovary :—*all magnified*

ICACINEÆ.

Stemonurus Vitiensis, Seem. Supra, p. 39.

This name must give way to *Lasianthera Vitiensis*, Seem., *Lasianthera* being the oldest generic name. Conf Benth et Hook f. Gen. vol i p 996.

ILICINEÆ.

Ilex Vitiensis, A. Gray. Supra, p. 40.

The stamens are not so sessile as drawn in A. Gray's plate, but on rather long filaments Is the drawing incorrect, or is Harvey's plant, on which I principally noticed the difference, a different species to that of A. Gray? In habit and other characters there does not seem to be any difference between the two.

SAPINDACEÆ.

Dodonæa viscosa, Linn. Supra, p. 49.—Viti, locality not specified (Harvey!)

LEGUMINOSÆ.

Erythrina Indica, Lam. Supra, p 60.

My var. β may possibly belong to *E. ovalifolia*, Roxb.

Cassia obtusifolia, Linn.   Supra, p. 67.—Viti, locality not specified (Harvey!).

Inocarpus edulis, Forst.   Supra, p. 70.—Viti, locality not specified (Harvey!).

Entada scandens, Benth.   Supra, p. 71.—Island of Lakeba (Harvey!)

ROSACEÆ.

Rubus tiliaceus, Smith.   Supra, p. 76—Viti, locality not specified (Harvey!)

This is rather a Bramble than a Raspberry, as I have called it.

MYRTACEÆ.

Cupheanthus, Seem.   Supra, p. 76—In adn :—

According to Brongniart and Gris (Bull. Soc. Bot. Fr. 1866, p. 170), *Gaslandia*, Vieill. in Bull. Soc. Linn. Norm. vol. x p. 96, is identical with this genus, my name having the priority. The genus is an anomalous one, and as its long tubular curved calyx reminded me of *Cuphea*, I named it *Cupheanthus*. At first I decided to place it in *Lythrarieæ*, and had actually the letterpress set up in that way, but finally determined to retain it in *Myrtaceæ*, chiefly on account of its inferior ovary, and certain features which it has in common with *Punica*, such as the thick valvate and coloured calyx, and the impunctate and subverticillate leaves I now find that Bentham and Hooker ('Genera Plantarum,' p. 696), whilst retaining *Cupheanthus* amongst the anomalous genera of *Myrtaceæ*, refer *Punica* to *Lythrarieæ*. In my mind there is no doubt that *Punica* and *Cupheanthus* are closely allied, and must be dealt with collectively ; and it is singular that we should have arrived independently at the same conclusion about their affinity. Unfortunately, the only specimen of *Cupheanthus* existing at the British Museum, is imperfect, but I think there is no doubt that the calyx is valvate ; I have never seen any calyx of the thickness of that of *Cupheanthus* that is imbricate, as the authors of the 'Genera Plantarum' suppose it to be. Recent investigations have almost completely broken down the boundary-line between *Myrtaceæ* and *Lythrarieæ* upon which systematists formerly used to rely.

Nelitris Vitiensis, A. Gray.   Supra, p. 80.—Viti, locality not specified (Harvey!).

Metrosideros polymorpha, Gaud.   Supra, p. 83.—Island of Lakeba (Harvey!).

MELASTOMACEÆ.

Naudinia, Dcne.   Supra, p. 86.

Bentham and Hooker (Gen. Plant. vol. i p. 771) refer this to *Astronia*, Blum.

RHIZOPHORACEÆ.

Crossostylis, Forst. Gen. p. 87. t. 41.   Calyx profunde 4-fidus, 4-angularis, lobis 3-angularibus æstivatione valvatis.   Petala 4, calyce inserta, ligulata, unguiculata, apice truncato 3-5-dentata, carinata, æstivatione involuta, decidua.   Stamina fertilia 20-28, margini libero disci perigyni inserta ; filamenta elongata, subulato-filiformia, basi dilatata, subconnata, intus glandula subglobosa instructa ; antheræ ovoideæ, introrsæ, 2-loculares, longitudinaliter dehiscentes ; filamenta sterilia fertilibus alterna, iisdem dimidio breviora, subulato-linearia, villosissima.   Stylus filiformis, elongatus, apice radiato 6-28-fidus ; lobis filiformibus, apice stigmatosis, in phalanges plus minus coadunatis. Ovarium depressum, calycis tubo semi-adnatum, vertice libero demum convexum, 6-28-radiatum, incomplete 6-28-loculare.   Ovula in loculis gemina, anatropa, e columna centrali appensa.   Fructus operculo hemisphærico striato dehiscens, incomplete 6-28-locularis, loculis 1-2-spermis —Arbusculæ glabræ ; foliis oppositis, obovatis, integerrimis v. subserrulatis ; stipulis interpetiolaribus, caducis ; pedunculis axillaribus, 1-4-floris ; floribus pedicellatis.—*Tomostyles*, Montr. in Mem. Acad. Lyon. vol. x. p. 201.

This genus has recently been augmented by several species, so that it is now composed of—1, *C biflora*, Forst. Char. Gen. p. 44, Prodr n 266, et Icon (ined) t 195, from the Society Islands (Forster! in Mus Brit) and Samoan group (U S Expl. Exped); 2, *C grandiflora*, Brongn. et Gris in Bull Soc Bot. Fr, Nov. 1863, p. 377, from New Caledonia (Vieillard and Pancher), 3, *C. multiflora*, Brongn et Gris l c, from New Caledonia (Vieillard, n 13), 4, *C. Harveyi*, Seem, from Viti (Harvey!), and probably a fifth species, which was also collected by Forster in the Society Islands, but which was not named by him, and which, at the British Museum, is mixed in one sheet with *C biflora*, and on another sheet bears the name *C biflora*, written by Pallas, through whose hands these specimens had passed before they were purchased by the British Museum This last species resembles my *C. Harveyi*, but the specimens are too imperfect to be described.

The following note on the genus, by Brongniart and Gris, extracted from the 'Bulletin de la Société Botanique de France,' 1863, is too important to be here omitted —

"The collections made by Messrs Pancher and Vieillard in New Caledonia include, in bud, flower, and fruit, a plant which we recognize as belonging to the genus somewhat imperfectly described by Forster as *Crossostylis*. The size of its flowers induced us to give it the specific name *grandiflora*, and M Pancher, in his last communication, has been led to give it the same name *Crossostylis biflora*, Forst, has been described and figured recently by Asa Gray in the Botany of Captain Wilkes' Voyage (U S Expl Exped p 610, t. 77), but he did not see it in fruit, and his description of the flower, when compared with specimens of this species, seems incorrect in a rather important point, relating to the structure of the ovary. *Crossostylis biflora* and *C grandiflora* agree in all essential points of structure; they differ slightly in the form of their sepals and petals, and the number of their stamens, viz twenty in *C biflora*, according to Forster and Asa Gray, though we noticed twenty-one to twenty-four in the flowers of a specimen of this species from New Caledonia, and twenty-eight in *C grandiflora*, one being in front of each petal, and six in front of each sepal. The same appendages are found at the base of the stamens within the calyx-tube. The ovary, which is plunged for half its length in the receptacle, and whose upper convex surface is marked with radiating striæ, has been described and figured by Asa Gray as having twelve cells with two ovules in each, Forster says the fruit is one-celled In examining carefully the ovary of the two species at our disposal, we ascertained clearly. even in young buds, that the partitions observed by the learned American botanist are nothing but elevated plates springing from the base and sides of the ovary, but which in a later stage are neither united with nor even close to the upper free wall of the ovary They are but incomplete partitions, prominent in *C biflora*, and not more than slightly prominent nerves in *C grandiflora* These laminæ, however, indicate the number of carpels constituting the ovary, to each of which correspond two ovules placed on the central column which runs through the ovary This column, at first very short, lengthens as the fruit grows, and as its upper surface becomes more convex The ovules, which at first are horizontal, are ultimately suspended at the ends of rather long stiff funiculi in the fertile seeds The stigma has as many small linear lobes as there are carpels, and these lobes, differently placed, are frequently united in four bundles, as Forster has observed The carpels in *C biflora* appear to be from twelve to sixteen, in *C. grandiflora* the number is equal to that of the stamens, viz twenty-eight. The fruit, which no one but Forster has described, seems to us to differ much from his description. That of *C grandiflora* externally much resembles Forster's figure, but it is not an indehiscent berry The upper convex part, forming a hemispherical lid, marked with radiating striæ, falls off after the rupture of the central column above the insertion of the seeds This central column, which remains in the middle of the base of the fruit, contains, in those we have seen, many abortive ovules and some fertile ripe seeds These last were suspended at the ends of stiff subulate funiculi, which ended in a white, spongy, lobed caruncle, partly covering the seed When this seed falls, the little cellular excrescence does not remain attached to it as an arillus, but to the funiculus The presence of these seminal appendages in a fruit with many fertile seeds would resemble pulp, and this led Forster to call this fruit 'bacca unilocularis polysperma.' The seed is oval, with a black, smooth, shining testa, the perisperm is fleshy, thick, and the straight embryo is axillary; its radicle is directed upwards towards the hilum, and its cotyledons, not broader than the young stem, are elliptical, convex, and applied to each other. These characters of the seed confirm the relation of this genus to *Legnotideæ* —Since this note was read, we have seen in M Vieillard's collection (No 43) a third species of *Crossostylis*, which we propose to call *C. multiflora* It differs from both the preceding species, firstly, by repeatedly forked peduncles, with much smaller flowers, secondly, by the much smaller number of the parts of the andrœcium and pistil, which are both reduced to eight, four stamens being opposite to the sepals and four to the petals "

C. Harveyi, (sp. nov) Seem.; glabra; ramulis crassis, nodosis, foliis obovatis v. ovalibus, obtusis retusisve, basi acutis, integerrimis, coriaceis; pedunculis 2- v. dichotome 4-floris; stylo 6-8-fido; ovario 6-8-radiato, incomplete 6-8-loculari —Viti, locality not specified (Harvey ! in Mus. Brit)

This species has smaller and more coriaceous leaves than *C biflora*, from Tahiti (Forster!) The branches are stout. Petiole ¼ inch long Blade 3–3½ inches long, 1½–2 inches broad, and quite glabrous on both sides Stamens numerous, but flowers too far advanced to allow of the counting of their exact number

COMBRETACEÆ.

Terminalia Catappa, Linn. P. 93, line 11 from above, read: "green" for "grey."

TACCACEÆ.

Tacca pinnatifida, Forst. Supra, p 102. Add as synonym *T. Oceanica*, Nutt, in Ann. Journ. of Pharm. vol. ix. cum icon. Seem Journ. of Bot. vol. iii p. 261, where I have been able to settle this point, through Professor A. Gray's kind offices.

Tacca maculata, Seem. Supra, p 103, line 24 from above, read: "but," instead of "and."

HEDERACEÆ.

Since I wrote the account of the Vitian members of this Order, I have completed my 'Revision of the Natural Order Hederaceæ,' with Illustrations, octavo; London, Reeve and Co, 1868. The whole Order is divided into five tribes, of which three are represented in Viti, viz.:—

Tribus I. HORSFIELDIEÆ.—Stamina petalorum numero æqualia. Ovarium 2-(per excessum 3-)merum Albumen æquabile.

Hydrocotyle, Linn., ex parte

Nothopanax, Miq, Seem.

Tribus II. PSEUDOPANACEÆ.—Stamina petalorum numero æqualia. Ovarium 5-∞ (abortu 3- nunquam 2-)merum. Albumen æquabile.

Agalma, Miq.

Schefflera, Forst.

Tribus III. PLERANDREÆ.—Stamina 2-∞ plo petalorum numero. Ovarium 5-∞-merum

Nesopanax, Seem.

Bakeria, Seem. (Stamens in this genus generally 15-23 in several rows.)

Plerandra, A. Gray.

CORNACEÆ.

Rhytidandra Vitiensis, A. Gray. Supra, p. 119.—Add as synonyms *Marlea Vitiensis*, Benth. Fl. Austr. vol iii. p. 386 *Pseudolangium polyosmoides*, F. Muell. Fragm. vol. ii. p. 84. *Rhytidandra polyosmoides*, F. Muell Frag vol. ii. p. 176.

According to Bentham, the genus *Rhytidandra* should be merged into *Marlea*, and this particular species, which is also found on the east coast of New Holland, should bear the name he has given to it.

LORANTHACEÆ.

Loranthus insularum, A. Gray. Supra, p. 120.—Nomen vernac. Vitiense, "Saburo."

The leaves are used by the natives for dyeing their cloth and cordage black

RUBIACEÆ.

Stylocoryne Harveyi, Seem. Supra, p 124—Nadi, Island of Vanua Levu (Harvey! in Mus. Brit.)

Tatea, Seem. Supra, p. 125, in adn. —

This name must give place to that of *Grisia*, Brongn., which has the right of priority by some months

[PUBLISHED JUNE 1, 1871.] 3 K

My *T. portlandioides*, which is n 850 (not, as by a misprint of mine, 890) of Vieillard's collection, is *G. campanulata*, Brongn. et Gris, in Bull. Soc Bot Fr 1865, p. 405

Lindenia, Benth. Supra, p. 128.

L Vitiensis, Seem , has been found by Dr Græffe in the Samoan Islands, and by the French collectors in New Caledonia, where also a second species (*L. Austro-Caledonica*, Brongn et Gris, Bull Soc Bot Fr 1865, p 407, et in Ann Sc Nat (Bot) 1866, p 258) has been met with by Pancher in 1862, and also by Vieillard (his n 651), so that now three species of this genus are known The American *L rivalis*, Benth , I have recently collected at Barquito, Port of Corinto, Nicaragua, and also on the Bayano River, Isthmus of Panama, the latter being the most southern station as yet recorded

Coffea Arabica, Linn. .

Coffee will one day rank amongst the staple products of Viti, the mountain slopes of Viti Levu, Vanua Levu, and Kadavu, and, above all, those of the valley of Namosi, being well adapted for its growth. Several old Coffee-trees I found in the Rewa district, showing the plant to be not of recent introduction Dr Brower, the American consul, established a plantation on his estate at Wakaya, and, at the time of my visit, the late Mr. Binner, of Levuka (Ovalau), had in his garden a number of thriving seedlings

Guettarda, Vent. Supra, p 131, read: "Ovula suspensa" instead of "erecto" in generic character. Conf. A. Gray, in Proceed Am. Acad.

COMPOSITÆ.

Myriogyne minuta, Less. Supra, p. 144.—Viti, locality not specified (Harvey !).

Sonchus asper, Vill. Supra, p. 145, line 7 from above, read: "disco utrinque tristriatis," instead of "disci utrinque triaristatis."

MYRSINEÆ.

Mæsa nemoralis, DC Supra, p. 148.—Viti, locality not specified (Harvey !).

Mæsa persicæfolia, A. Gray. Supra, p. 148.—Viti, locality not specified (Harvey !).

JASMINEÆ.

Jasminum australe, Pers Supra, p. 154.

Bentham (Fl. Austr. vol iii p 296), who adopts all my synonyms of this species, which should bear Forster's (the oldest) name of *J simplicifolium*, also refers to it *J. acuminatum*, R Brown, Prodr 521, *J. confusum*, DC Prodr vol. viii. p. 309, and with some hesitation *J. funale*, Dene Herb Tim p 77.

APOCYNEÆ.

Tabernæmontana orientalis, R Br. Supra, p. 159

Bentham (Fl. Austr vol iv. p 311) has some remarks on the synonymy of this plant, he believing it distinct from either *T orientalis*, R. Br , and *T. Cumingiana*, De Cand. At first I held the same opinion, and gave the name of *T Vitiensis* to my Viti plant, but Asa Gray referred it (' Bonplandia,' 1862, p 37), though with hesitation, to *T Cumingiana* I reconsidered the subject, and ultimately adopted the synonymy given above

Alstonia villosa, Seem. Supra, p. 161.

There being an *A villosa* of Blume, I now name my plant *A. Vitiensis*

ASCLEPIADEÆ.

Hoya Samoensis, Seem. Supra, p. 163.

The Samoan vernacular name of this plant is "Fue-ele-la" See Powell in Journ. of Botany, 1868, p 278 seq , for an account of this and other Samoan plants.

GENTIANEÆ.

I have lately found in Nicaragua a genus of *Gentianeæ* with irregular (green) flowers, which modifies the ordinal character.

Limnanthemum Kleinianum, Griseb. Supra, p. 167.—Viti, locality not specified (Harvey!).

Bentham (Fl Austr. vol. iii. p. 167) refers this plant to *L. Indicum*, Thw., and does not think that any importance can be attached to the fact, whether the seeds be muricate or not. I could not find smooth and muricate seeds on the same individual

BORAGINEÆ.

Cordia dichotoma, Forst. Supra, p. 168.

Bentham (Fl Austr) refers this, I think rightly, to *C. Myxa*, Linn., adding as synonyms *C. Browni*, DC., *C. latifolia*, Roxb, and *C irtocarpa*, F. Muell

CONVOLVULACEÆ.

A. Gray (in Mann's Enum. Hawaiian Plants, p 195) gives the name of *Ipomæa Forsteri* to *Ipomæa carnea*, of Forst, but no character. He refers to it my n 328, which I had called *I sepiaria*

Calonyction speciosum, Chois. Supra, p. 171. Add: Common in tropical Australia (F. Mueller!).

Pharbitis insularis, Chois. Supra, p 171.

Bentham identifies this with *Ipomæa congesta*, R Br (*Convolvulus congestus*, Spr.)

Ipomœa denticulata, Chois. Supra, p 172.

Bentham agrees with me in holding the doubtful *I carnea*, Forst, non Jacq, identical with this species

Aniseia uniflora, Chois. Supra, p 173.—Viti, locality not specified (Harvey!). Also in tropical New Holland (F. Mueller!).

SOLANEÆ.

Solanum xanthocarpum, Schrad. Supra, p. 174.

This is, according to H Mann, *S aculeatissimum*, Jacq Col. vol. i. p. 100, et Icon. Rar. vol. i. tab. 11, not *S xanthocarpum* of Schrad

Solanum tetrandrum, R. Brown. Supra, p. 176.—Isle of Viwa (Harvey!).

Solanum repandum, Forst. Supra, p 177.—Isle of Viwa (Harvey!).

Nicotiana suaveolens, Lehm. Supra, p. 179.

Bentham (Fl Austr. vol iii p. 169) adds the following synonyms to this species,—*H rotundifolia*, Lindl, and *H. fastigiata*, Nees, but he overlooks some of the synonyms, which I referred to it from authentic specimens

SCROPHULARINEÆ.

Herpestris. Supra, p. 180, read: *H. Monniera* instead of *Moniera*.

ACANTHACEÆ.

Adenosma. Supra, p. 184, line 2 from below, read · "triflora" instead of "tiflora."

Eranthemum. Supra, p 185. To list of Polynesian species add: *E. asperum*, Hook. f. Bot. Mag. t 5711; and, line 17 from below, 5467, instead 4467.

E asperum, Hook f, is closely allied to *E. repandum*, which has, however, broader, ovate or ovate-oblong leaves, deeper cut at edge, peduncles 2–3-florous only; lobes of corolla more acute; and lower lobes less marked with purple.

VERBENACEÆ.

Faradaya. Supra, p. 188.

A new species of this was found by Powell in the Samoan Islands, viz *F. Powelli*, Seem Journ of Bot 1868.

LABIATEÆ.

Ocimum gratissimum, Linn. Supra, p. 191.—Island of Lakeba (Harvey!).

Teucrium inflatum, Sw. Supra, p. 193.—Viti, locality not specified (Harvey!).

LAURACEÆ.

An additional Polynesian member of this Order was collected in the Hawaiian Islands (*Oreodaphne Kaauensis*, Mann; Statistics and Geogr Range of Hawaiian Plants, in Seem Journ Bot 1869, p 177)

THYMELÆACEÆ.

Wikstrœmia fœtida, var. **Vitiensis,** A. Gray.

According to Powell, the "Mati" of the Samoan group is not this plant, but a species of the genus *Ficus*.

EUPHORBIACEÆ.

Phyllanthus ramiflorus, Mull. Arg. Supra, p. 218.—Viti, locality not specified (Harvey!).

Acalypha Wilkesiana, Mull. Arg Supra, p. 225.

This has lately been observed in New Caledonia. I introduced it into our gardens, where it is now a great favourite on account of its foliage

Acalypha insulana, Mull. Arg. Supra, p. 225 —Viti, locality not specified (Harvey!).

URTICACEÆ.

Sponia velutina, Planch. Supra, p. 235.—Nadi, Island of Vanua Levu (Harvey!).

Laportea Vitiensis, Seem Supra, p. 239.

Weddell (De Cand Prodr vol xvi sect i p. 83) united this with the allied *L photiniphylla*, Wedd, though the venation of the leaves is altogether different

Pellionia filicoides, Seem. Supra, p. 239.

This plant Weddell has enumerated twice in De Candolle's Prodr. l. c , at p 168 under *Pellionia*, and at p 188, under *Elatostema* He thinks *P. Vitiensis*, A Gray, which I referred as a synonym to this species, holding the specimen of it in the Kew herbarium to be a young plant, to be a distinct species, though closely allied Until more specimens come to hand, the point cannot be decided satisfactorily.

P. 240, after **Pellionia filicoides,** add.

3 **Pellionia australis,** Wedd. in De Cand. Prodr. vol. xvi. sect i. p. 169, dioica; foliis sub-oppositis admodumque disparibus, in quoque jugo altero amplo elliptico subabrupte et anguste acuminato basi obtuso v. acuminato fere in toto margine inæqualiter serrato 3-plinervio nervis subtus hirtulis, altero abortivo minimo fere deltoideo seu acute 3-lobo; cymis ♂ densifloris, pedunculatis, pedunculo quam petiolus folii majoris longiore —Island of Ovalau (Vieillard) in Herb Lenormand.

Cypholophus macrocephalus, Wedd Supra, p. 243

The Samoan name of this plant is "O le Fau pata," not "O le Tau pata," as misspelt, and one kind of fine mat made of the bark of this species is called "Ie-sina" (not "Jesina," or "je-sina," as incorrectly written by me).

Weddell (De Cand. Prodr vol xvi sect i. p. 235/11) separates one of his varieties of *C. macro-phyllus* (viz *heterophyllus*, my *Bœhmeria Harveyi*) as a distinct species, which he terms *C. heterophyllus,* Wedd

Pipturus velutinus, Wedd. Supra, p. 243.—Nadi, Island of Vanua Levu (Harvey!).

P. 244, **Pipturus,** add:

3. **Pipturus platyphyllus,** Wedd. in De Cand. Prodr. vol xvi. sect. i. p. 235/19; ramulis hirtis demumque glabratis; foliis amplis, ovatis, acuminatis, basi rotundatis, crenato-serratis, concoloribus, supra asperato-hispidis, subtus molliter pubescentibus; glomerulis in spicas simplices interruptas digestis.—Island of Ovalau (Vieillard in Herb Lenormand).

4. **Pipturus gracilipes,** A. Gray in litt. Wedd. l. c. Species indescripta.—Viti (U. S. Expl. Exped).

Missiessya corymbulosa, Wedd. Supra, p. 244 —Viti, locality not specified (Harvey!).

Weddell (De Cand l c) refers this to the genus *Leucosyke*, under the name *L corymbulosa*, Wedd.

Maouttia australis, Wedd. Supra, p 245.

The Samoan name of this plant should be written "O le Faunuta," instead of "O le Faunuta," as above

Ficus tinctoria, Forst. Supra, p. 249.

By mistake the *plate* representing this species is numbered 73 instead of 63.

Trophis anthropophagorum, Seem. Supra, p. 258.

By mistake the *plate* representing this species is numbered 63 instead of 73

PIPERACEÆ.

Peperomia pallida, A. Dietr. Supra, p. 259.

Casimir de Candolle (Prodr vol xvi. sect i p 158) separates my n 565 from this, under the name of *P Vitiana*, though I convinced him, in our correspondence on the subject, that the characters he relied on broke down, and in the last revise sheet I finally expunged the name *P. Vitiana P. Oahuensis,* Cas. de Cand, may also belong to this species as a synonym.

CONIFERÆ.

Gnetum, Linn. Mant. p. 125; Parlat. in DC. Prodr. Sec. ii. p. 348. Flores monoici v. rarius dioici. Amenta axillaria, raro etiam terminalia, solitaria vel 2-plura, fasciculato-conferta, simplicia v. subracemosa, cylindracea, articulata, interrupte verticillata, verticillis singulis bracteis in discum sive involucrum peltatum simul connatis cinctis. Flores palcis setaceo-laceris, laciniis filiformibus articulatis (bracteolis) immersi, nunc ♂ et ♀ in eodem verticillo mixti, nunc in verticillos diversos v. in amenta propria interdum in diversa stirpe segregati. Fl. ♂ bracteolati; bracteolæ 2, simul connatæ, involucellum 2-valve efformantes. Stamen 1 e fundo involucelli ortum. Filamentum simplex v. rarissime apice aut profunde? 2-fidum. Anthera 2-locularis, didyma, loculis contiguis v. in filamenti cruribus sejunctis, apice rima transversa demum porro dehiscentibus Fl. ♀· Involucellum 0. Pistillum 1, erectum, bracteolatum. Bracteolæ 4, per paria oppositæ et coalitæ, urceolum duplex utrumque apice pro emissione styli perforatum et pistillum includens efformantes. Ovarium ovoideum v. oblongum. Stylus longus, filiformis. Stigma fimbriatum. Fructus urceolis succulentis v. rigide coriaceis spurie drupaceus v. uucamentaceus. Embryo in apice albuminis dense carnosi subclavatus, cotyledonibus 2 minimis denticuliformibus, radicula in filum longissimum flexuoso-intricatum desinente.—Frutices sarmentosi, rarius arbores erectæ. Ram i oppositi, geniculato-nodosi. Folia opposita, coriacea, petiolata, petiolis supra sulco longitudinaliter exaratis et basi connatis, ovata vel ovalia aut ovali-oblonga, integerrima, penninervia.

1 **G. Gnemon,** Linn. Mant p 125; arbor monoica; ramis articulato-nodosis; foliis oppositis breviter petiolatis elliptico-oblongis vel ellipticis apice subacuminatis basi attenuatis, amentis solitariis vel paucis subumbellatis aut raro vix racemosis, rachide inferne nuda; floribus crebre verticillato-capitatis, verticillis subglobosis, drupis subsessilibus (rubris) ovali oblongis, obtusis cum mucronulo.—Parlatore, l. c.; Blume! Nov. Pl Fm. p 30 et in Ann des Sc Nat. 2 série, t. 2 p. 105. et Rumph. vol iv. p 3. t. 176, Brongn. ad Duperr. p 6. t. 1; Endl Conif p 250; Carr. Conif. p. 536. *Gnemon domestica,* Rumph. Amb. vol. i. p. 181. t 71, 72.

Var. *β. sylvestris;* foliis minoribus, drupis obtusioribus —*Gnemon sylvestris,* Rumph Amb vol. i p 183 t. 73. *Gnetum ovalifolium,* Poir Suppl. vol. ii. p. 810 *G. sylvestre,* Brongn. ad Duperr. p. 12. *G Gnemon,* var. *β ovalifolium,* Blume, l. c., Endl. l. c.; Carr. l. c —Nadi, Island of Vanua Levu (Harvey! in Herb. Mus Brit).

This appears to be the most southerly station of the genus as yet recorded.

LEMNACEÆ.

Lemna minor, Linn   Supra, p 288

Hegelmaier (*Lemnaceæ,* 1868), p. 139, points out that this species is not *L minor* of Linnæus, but *L paucicostata,* Hegelm t 8 As yet it has not been found in Polynesia beyond Viti, nor in any part of Australia, though in many parts of the other continents

Lemna melanorrhiza, Kunze. Supra, p. 288.

It is regarded by Hegelmaier, l c, as a species of *Spirodela,* viz *S oligorrhiza,* Hegelm var *β melanorrhiza* Hegelm l c, p 148

GRAMINEÆ.

Schizostachyum glaucifolium, Munro Supra, p. 323, line 19 from below, add after Nomen vernac. Vitiense, the word "Bitu" and a full-stop.

INDEX.

PRINTED BY TAYLOR AND CO, LITTLE QUEEN STREET, LINCOLN'S INN FIELDS

W. Fitch del et lith.   Vincent Brooks Imp.

Polyalthia vitiensis Seem (sp nov)

Tab. VI

Calysaccion tinctorium, Seem.

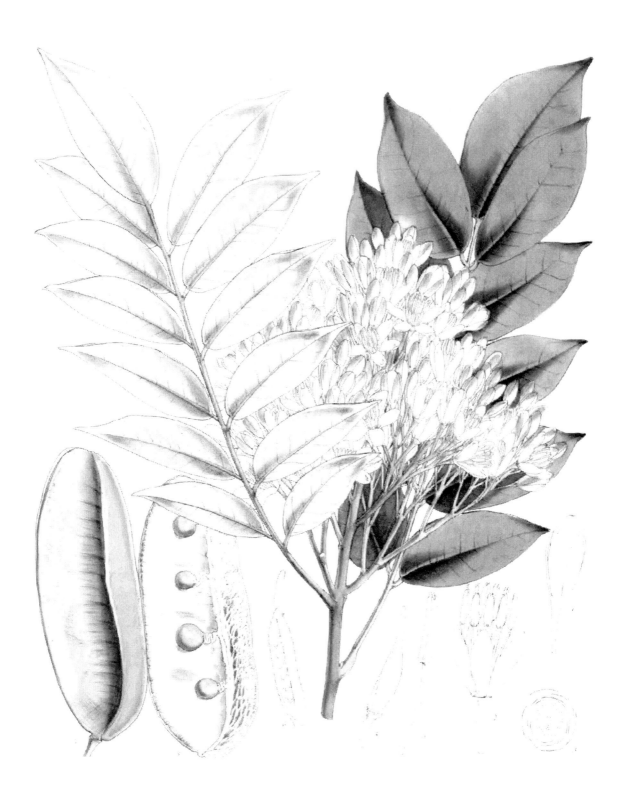

Cyrtanthemum Kaulsusia, Seem. t. ...

Nothopegia trifoliata

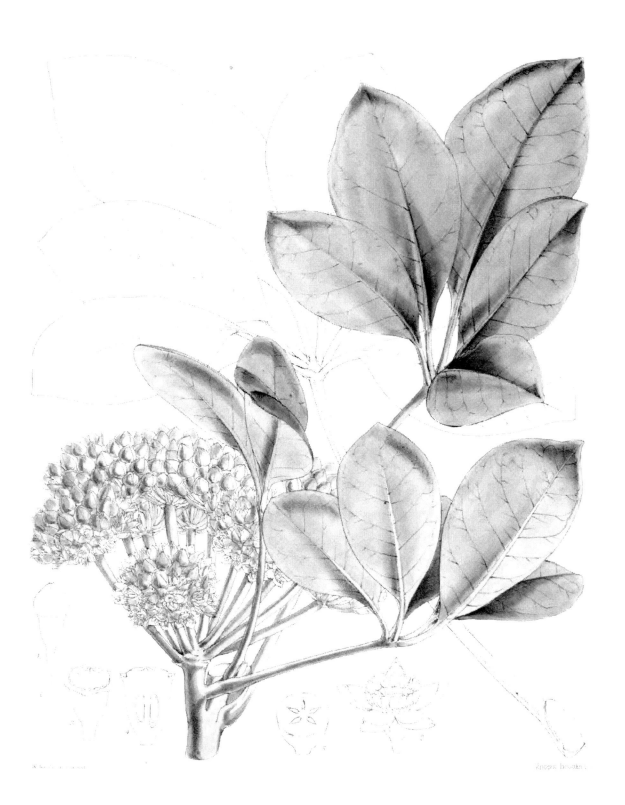

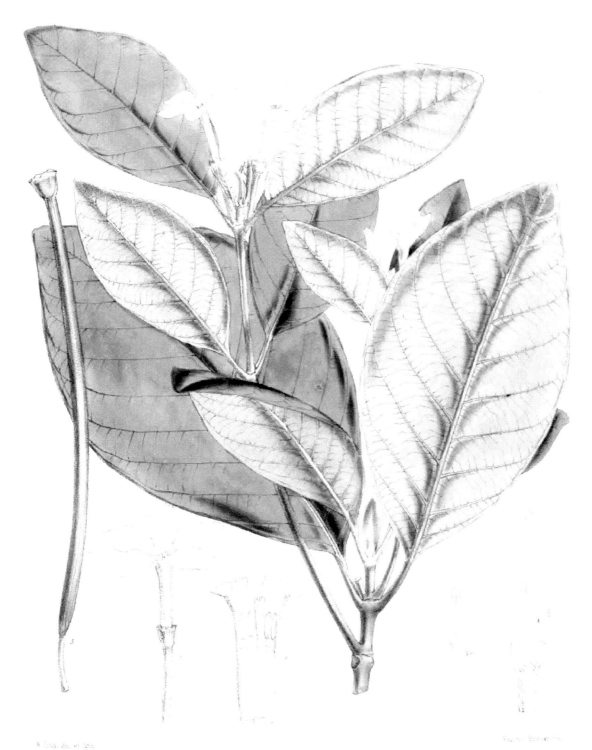

Pithecolobium longissimum Seem. (sp. nov.)

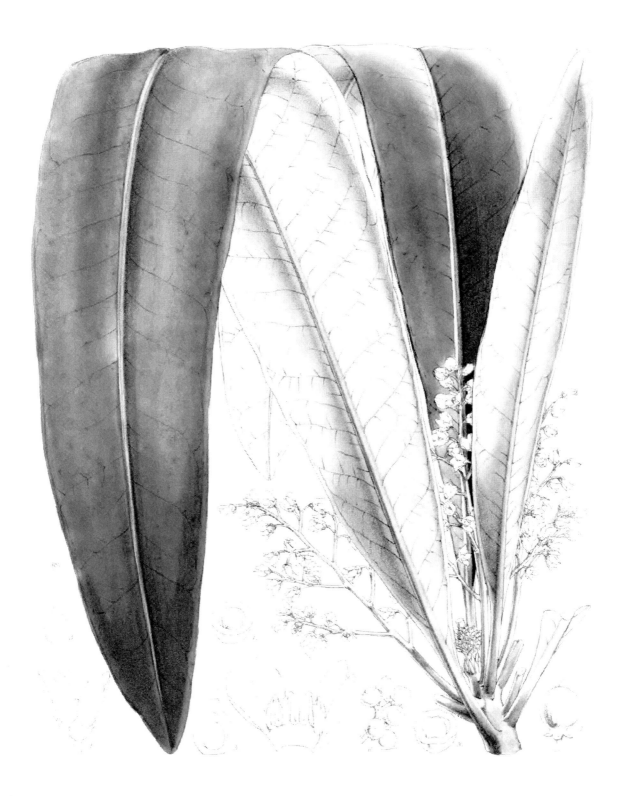

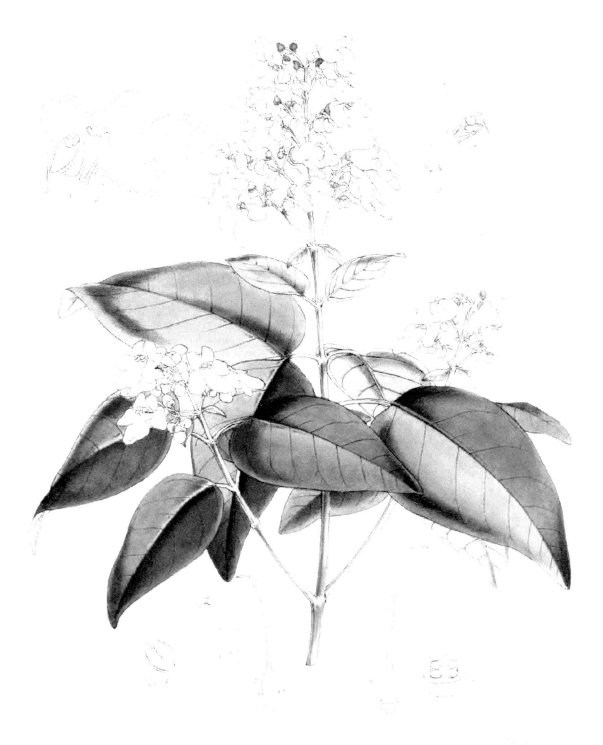

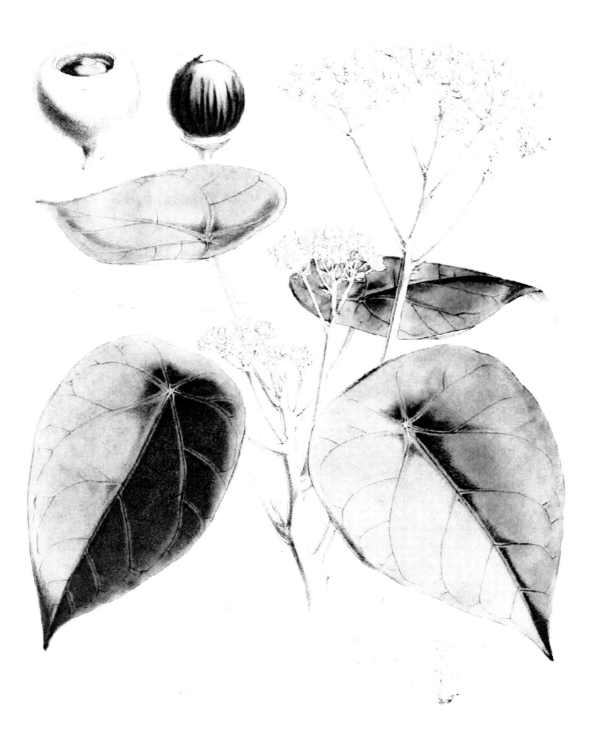

Dryplospermum zeylanicum, Gaertn. 3.

Croton Perrottetii var. ovata. Müll arg.

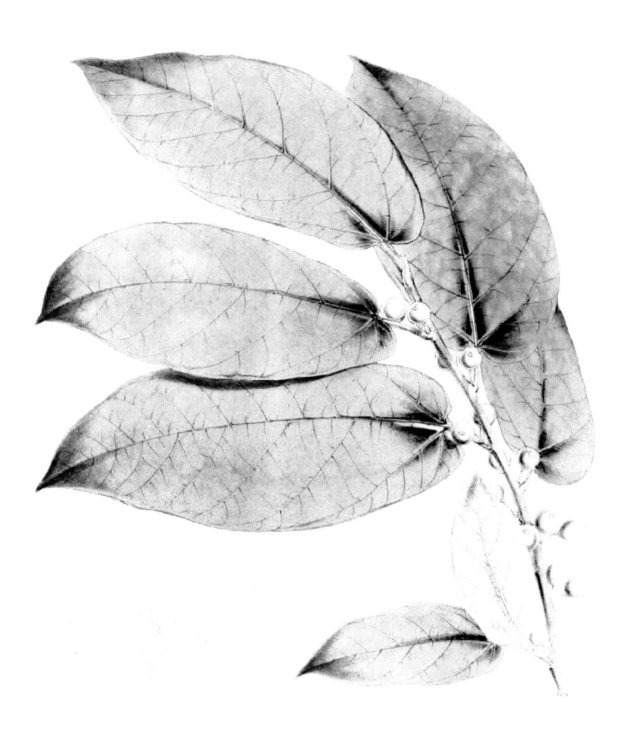

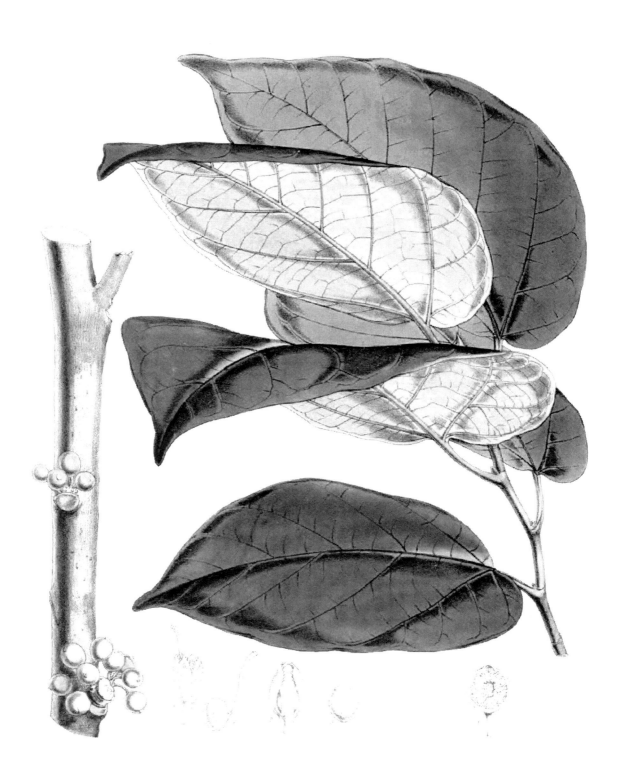

Podocarpus Mannii sp. n. Hook.

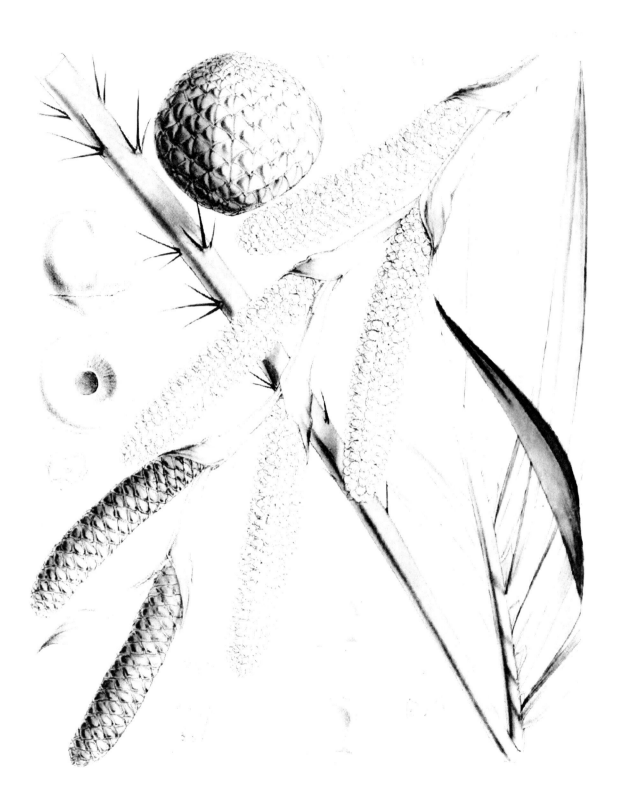

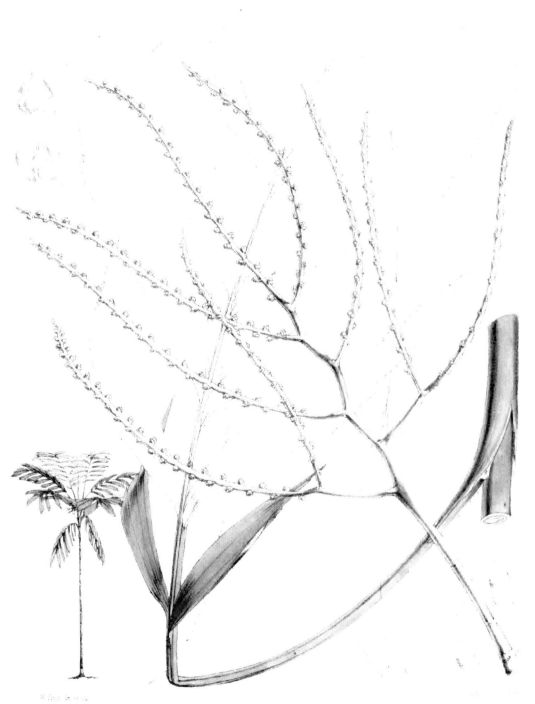

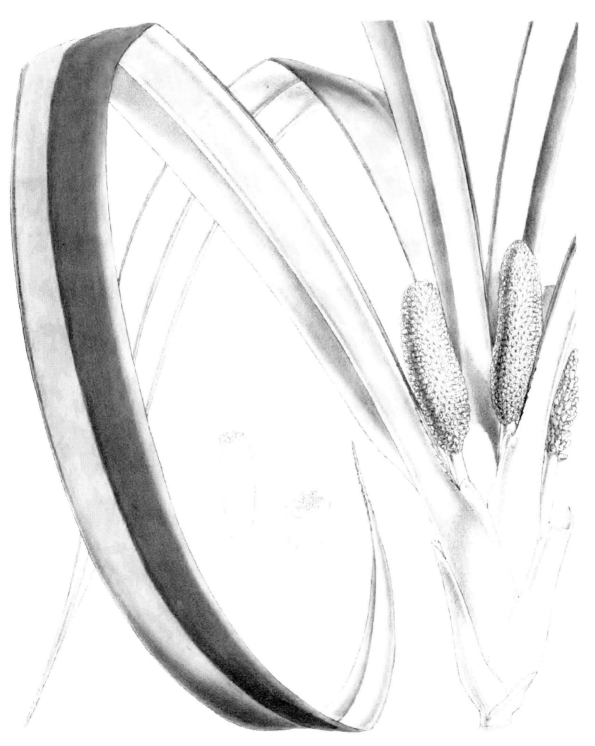

Amomum ......

W. Fitch del. et lith.

Dracaena septaria Bean (W. d.)

CPSIA information can be obtained at www.ICGtesting.com
Printed in the USA
BVOW07s0919110314

347293BV00010B/634/P